Remembering Fromelles

Remembering Fromelles

A new cemetery for a new century

Compiled by Julie Summers

Julie Summers is an historian specialising in the two World Wars. Author of nine books, including *Remembered, The History of the Commonwealth War Graves Commission* (2007), she worked for twenty years in various capacities in the European art world before becoming a full-time writer. She has travelled widely in Europe, Australia and the Far East.

Contents

In May 2007 we celebrated the ninetieth anniversary of the founding of the Commonwealth War Graves Commission with a book and exhibition that showed not only our work in the past but our aims for the future.

Just one year later a number of mass graves were found at Pheasant Wood, near Fromelles in northern France, the site of a disastrous battle on 19/20 July 1916. The Australian and British governments asked the Commission to oversee the project to remove and, where possible, identify the 250 remains buried in the six graves and to construct a new cemetery close by in order to give them the dignity and honour in death which has been denied them for 93 years.

This enormous undertaking has been completed in a very short space of time and in a spirit of cooperation between all parties. Every person who has played a role has felt privileged to have been involved and I am grateful to each of them for carrying out their tasks so professionally.

For nearly forty years I have witnessed at first-hand the work of the Commonwealth War Graves Commission and I am immensely proud of what we have achieved. To have constructed a new cemetery over half a century since the last one was built following the Second World War was entirely unforeseen but has proved that the Commission's work is as relevant today as it was at its foundation ninety years ago.

This book celebrates a great achievement in our long and distinguished history, bringing honour at last, more than three generations later, to those who died in the service of their country.

HRH The Duke of Kent, KG
President
Commonwealth War Graves Commission

Introduction

Julie Summers

In May 2008, after several years of painstaking research and investigation, a number of mass graves dating from the First World War were identified at Pheasant Wood, near Fromelles in northern France. They contained the remains of Australian and British servicemen who died in the Battle of Fromelles that took place between 19 and 20 July 1916.

For reasons of hygiene and decency, the men had been buried by the Germans soon after the battle. There they remained, undiscovered, for nearly a century until an Australian historian convinced military authorities that they were there.

The British and Australian Governments asked the Commonwealth War Graves Commission to oversee the operation to recover the remains and rebury them. Although remains of soldiers still come to light from the Great War at a rate of some 30 a year, the discovery of 250 bodies at one site was exceptional. It led to the decision that for the first time since the 1960s a new cemetery would have to be constructed by the Commission.

This commemorative publication charts the story of the discovery of the mass graves, the archaeology behind the excavations, the question of identification and the process of reburial and cemetery construction undertaken during the course of 2009 and 2010. The purpose of the whole undertaking has been to give these men the dignity in death they were denied for nearly a century but which, in keeping with the Commission's own founding beliefs, they so richly deserve.

It is perhaps useful to set out here how burials were carried out during and in the immediate aftermath of the Great War and in turn this will help to explain the role played by the then Imperial (now Commonwealth), War Graves Commission.

In May 1917, a remarkable organisation was granted Royal Charter: the Imperial War Graves Commission (which was renamed the Commonwealth War Graves Commission in 1960 to reflect the changing times). It was the creation of one man, Sir Fabian Ware. Neither a soldier nor a politician, Ware devoted his life from 1914 to his death in 1949 to the commemoration of the Commonwealth war dead.

Prior to the war, Ware had enjoyed a successful career in education and newspapers in both South Africa and Britain. Too old to fight, in 1914 he volunteered to command a fleet of volunteer drivers for the Red Cross in France. They were tasked with taking the wounded to hospital and picking up stragglers. Thousands of soldiers died in the intense fighting and he began to see graves and little cemeteries springing up all over the Western Front.

He and his men became concerned that these graves were not being properly recorded and he knew that this would cause distress to the families of the fallen in the future. Although the regiments made lists and notes about where men were buried there was no organisation responsible for ensuring that graves were maintained nor, more importantly, that the information on the temporary crosses or markers was recorded centrally. So he began to undertake this work in his capacity as a Red Cross official.

Over the course of the next two years, Ware's unit became recognised by the Army and praised by Field Marshall Sir Douglas Haig, as the unit responsible for the locating, recording, photographing and care of soldiers' graves in France and Belgium. So successful was their work and of such value to the morale of the soldiers in the field and to the relatives back home that the work

opposite Bucquoy Road Cemetery, France 1920s, prior to handover to the Commission

above Major General Sir Fabian Ware KCVO, KBE, CB, CMG (17 June 1869 – 29 April 1949)

was extended to places far away from Britain: in Palestine, in Mesopotamia (Iraq), in the Dardanelles and in Italy.

Throughout the First World War, military burials were the responsibility of the Army in the field. In the less dangerous areas they would be undertaken by burial parties made up of men from pioneer or labour units under the direction of an appointed burial officer and an army chaplain. Most of these burials would be made in reasonably well-established burial grounds, often attached to dressing stations, casualty clearing stations or field hospitals. The grave would be marked with a wooden cross bearing the casualty's details and a careful note made of the position of the burial.

In times of advance or heavy fighting, field burials could not be so easily regulated. Frequently, they were carried out in isolated positions by front line troops in haste, often under cover of night and under fire. Again, the grave would be marked with a peg or, if none was available, with a written note placed inside a tin or bottle that was pushed down into the grave. The exact position of the burial would be noted with the aid of a large-scale map.

In both circumstances, details of the death and burial would be sent to the appropriate military authorities, including the Directorate of Graves Registration and Enquiries.

The DGR&E had been established in 1916 by Ware. It was an army organisation staffed by military personnel (usually those deemed too old or unfit for active service) and responsible to the military authorities. In simple terms, its responsibilities were to keep records of burials, to lay out and maintain burial grounds and to negotiate with the authorities for the land which the cemeteries occupied. It also dealt with

above Battlefield burials at Maple Copse in Belgium

right Bethune Town Cemetery, France

above Fauquissart Military Cemetery, France in 1925 prior to construction by the Commission's architect, W.H. Cowlishaw

above Men of the
Graves Registration Unit
unearthing remains

below A funeral at
Tyne Cot Cemetery,
Belgium, in the 1920s

Western Front had been given a proper
burial in a designated military cemetery
and the landscape was strewn with hundreds
of hastily made soldiers' cemeteries which
were often little more than clusters of graves
beside a road or canal. Ware's work with
the Graves Registration Unit helped to
identify known burial sites and there were
thousands of isolated graves in the battle
areas but of course countless bodies still
remained unburied in what had been
No Man's Land which the GCUs had been
unable to reach.

As the work to clear the battlefields
progressed, so Ware's vision of
commemoration for the fallen began to be
realised. He brought together a powerful
group of experts in various fields, including
Sir Edwin Lutyens, Reginald Blomfield and
Herbert Baker, who were appointed leading
architects on the Western Front, with
Sir Robert Lorimer responsible for Italy and
Greece and Sir John James Burnet working
further afield in Palestine and Gallipoli.
Gertrude Jekyll and Arthur Hill, Assistant
Director at Kew Gardens, amongst others
advised on horticulture, while Sir William
Garstin, the engineer of the Aswan Dam,
was also a Commissioner. He had lost a
son in the early years of the Great War, as
had Rudyard Kipling who was appointed
literary adviser to the Commission. Kipling's
influence is still felt in the language of
mourning engraved on the Commission's
headstones and memorials. It was Kipling
who chose the expression for Lutyens' great
Stone of Remembrance: 'Their Name Liveth
For Evermore', and for the headstone of
the soldiers who could not be identified:
'Known Unto God'.

The man charged by Ware to pull all
the advice together and to produce a vision
of how a war cemetery should look was

enquiries about casualties and administered
a service, funded by the Red Cross, whereby
photographs of graves were sent to grieving
families.

Soon Ware realised that recording the
graves was not enough. They needed to be
tended and cared for. He established the
National Committee for the Care of Soldiers'
Graves, which helped to convince others
that a separate organisation to deal with the
whole issue of commemoration would be
required. This led, in 1917, to the founding
of the Imperial War Graves Commission,
with backing at the highest level and with
the Prince of Wales as its first president.

After the Armistice, the systematic job
of clearing the battlefields of human remains
began. This was undertaken by special
units formed within the Army, called Graves
Concentration Units. Theirs was a grim
but vital task. Barely half the dead on the

Lieutenant Colonel Sir Frederic Kenyon, Director of the British Museum. Kenyon had served with the Inns of Court Regiment during the war and in 1917 he made visits to the battlefields of France and Belgium to see for himself the size of the Commission's task. By the time he delivered his report, in February 1918, the basic tenets of the Commission's philosophy were outlined. There should be no hierarchy of race, rank or creed. Every man was to be treated equally, a radical departure from what had gone before when, by and large, soldiers' remains would be buried in mass graves and officers only accorded individual burials and memorials if their regiment or family would pay for it. The headstone for each individual grave would be uniform in size and design, thus each man would be accorded the same respect. It would be funded by the member governments of

the Empire. Ware wrote in 1925: 'These dead deserved the honour which had been shown in this way to the former great of the earth, and as they could not be brought in their hundreds of thousands beneath the sacred shelter of existing monuments, structures at least as lasting must be erected at the spots in distant lands where their comrades buried them.'

Sir Frederic Kenyon described in his report of January 1918 how the cemeteries should look: 'The general appearance of a British cemetery,' he wrote, 'will be that of an enclosure with plots of grass or flowers (or both) separated by paths of varying size, and set with orderly rows of headstones, uniform in height and width. Shrubs and trees will be arranged in various places, sometimes as clumps at the junctions of ways, sometimes as avenues along the sides of the principal paths, sometimes around

top left **Le Trou Aid Post Cemetery, France designed by Sir Herbert Baker**

top right **Rudyard Kipling, literary adviser to the Commission**

above **Rue-du-Bacquerot No 1. Military Cemetery, France before headstone installation**

the borders of the cemetery. The graves will, wherever possible, face towards the east, and at the eastern end of the cemetery will be a great altar stone, raised upon broad steps, and bearing some brief and appropriate phrase or text. Either over the stone, or elsewhere in the cemetery, will be a small building where visitors may gather for shelter or for worship, and where the register of the graves will be kept. And at some prominent spot will rise the Cross, as the symbol of the Christian faith and of the self-sacrifice of the men who now lie beneath its shadow.'

Sir Frederic Kenyon's vision of a war cemetery is so remarkably similar to what is seen all over the world today that it is hard to remember that what confronted him visually in 1917 was a scene of such gargantuan destruction and horror as to defy the imagination. In place of the quiet cemeteries with orderly rows of white

headstones facing the Cross of Sacrifice he saw shell holes, barbed wire, trees blasted to shreds and overall the detritus of battle and hundreds of thousands of ad hoc burials.

Nearly a hundred years later, the same degree of care and respect has been shown to the 250 Australian and British servicemen who were buried by the Germans in 1916 and whose mass graves were not discovered in the Graves Concentration Units' extensive searches of the Fromelles area in 1919 and 1921. As in the early twentieth century, it is not the Commission that deals with the remains of the soldiers but an expert team, this time of archaeologists practiced in the recovery of remains from mass graves. Although some of the techniques used by Oxford Archaeology such as DNA sampling and x-rays, were not available to the units in 1919, much of the detailed examination of clues and artefacts is similar. Once again,

every item discovered with a body is carefully labelled and attempts are made to piece together the century-old jigsaw, which might lead to the identification of one or another man, and thus bring some closure to his family. The Commission's role has been, as before, a coordinating one and, eventually, a commemorative one as the cemetery is completed, the burials carried out and the planting and headstones installed.

left Le Trou Aid Post Cemetery is one of the closest to Fromelles and was established in 1914

right Fromelles (Pheasant Wood) Military Cemetery, France

The Missing Dead of Fromelles

Nigel Steel

Nigel Steel is Principal Historian for the Lord Ashcroft Gallery Project at the Imperial War Museum in London. From September 2006 to August 2008 he was a Visiting Senior Historian at the Australian War Memorial and a member of the Australian Army History Unit's second panel of investigation. From 2002 to 2004 he was also co-secretary of the All Party War Graves and Battlefield Heritage Group. He is the author of a number of books about the First World War.

Part I: The Battle

'I think the attack ... has done both divisions a great deal of good.'
Lieutenant General Sir Richard Haking, commander of XI Corps.

There is something about the battle of Fromelles, something nihilistic, that both fascinates and abhors us. For many years, historians have been researching and revising their opinions about the First World War. The popular view of 'lions led by donkeys' has largely been cast aside in favour of a more balanced understanding of the technical challenges and enormous scale that faced those who conducted the first industrial war of the twentieth century. A learning curve was followed by many senior figures, up to and including Field Marshal Sir Douglas Haig, the Commander-in-Chief himself. As they made mistakes, they learned a series of painful lessons that led them to develop the expertise and competence needed to command and successfully lead the largest army Britain and its Empire ever put into the field. This revision of our historical understanding cannot be applied to Fromelles. For historians it was, and remains, an unmitigated disaster. No tentative lessons or any kind of positive outcome can be

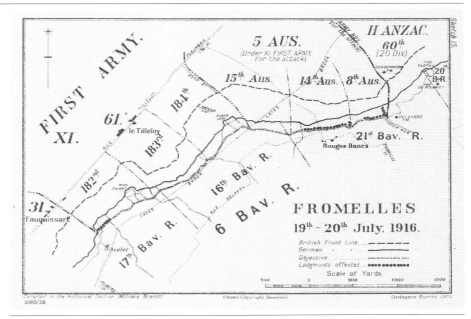

claimed for the 'battle' that took place in the area between the villages of Fromelles and Fleurbaix in northern France on 19 and 20 July 1916. It truly was the First World War at its worst.

Throughout the First World War Britain stood shoulder to shoulder on the Western Front with its foremost ally, France. It was a coalition war and for the first two years Britain was the junior partner. From the outbreak of the war in August 1914 until the middle of 1916, by and large the British fought where and when the French wanted. At the end of 1915 it was agreed that the major Franco-British offensive of the following year would be undertaken in Picardy, astride the river Somme. When the Germans launched their massive attack on the French fortress of Verdun in February 1916, the balance of the Somme offensive gradually began to tilt in favour of the

***opposite* Aerial photograph of the Fromelles battlefield looking south-east across the Australian trenches to the German front line with the Sugarloaf bottom right**

***above* Map of Fromelles showing the lines held by the British, Australian and German units involved, taken from the British Official History**

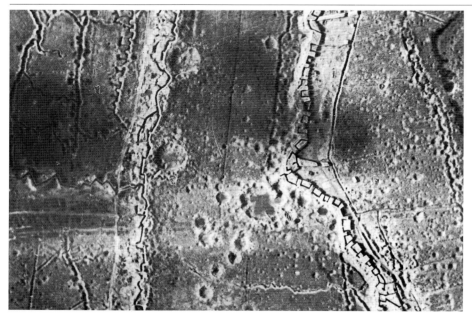

GHQ quickly scaled down pressure for a significant attack in the north. Instead, a plan emerged based on a proposal made by Lieutenant General Sir Richard Haking, commander of XI Corps, to assault and capture Aubers Ridge. Scaled down, Haking's plan was reconfigured as a limited, local attack. Supported by weak and largely inexperienced artillery units, one British and one Australian infantry division would assault the German front along a line roughly 4000m wide. Set into the German front were two recognised strong points where resistance was likely to be particularly fierce. In the centre was the strong point known as the Sugarloaf and in the south-west the strong point called the Wick Salient. Unfortunately, No Man's Land was at its greatest depth around the Sugarloaf, stretching for over 400m, and the intense, well-directed fire from this feature cut

British under Haig. They would now play the dominant role there.

The Battle of the Somme began on 1 July 1916 and continued for another 141 days. It became one of the defining episodes of the First World War. Between July and November 1916 the British Expeditionary Force (BEF) suffered almost 420,000 casualties on the Somme. The pain and trauma of the battle reached out into almost every town across Britain and the countries of its Empire. Yet, three weeks into this cataclysmic event another, much smaller, battle took place a short distance further north. Although of far less significance and consequence than the Somme, it too sent shock waves reverberating out into thousands more homes.

Fromelles was not really even a battle. It was a diversionary action fought by two infantry divisions, one from Britain, the

other from Australia, in the lowlands of French Flanders. Its stated objective was to breach the German lines in front of the barely perceptible Aubers Ridge, which had been assaulted many times before in the war, including during the main operation to capture it on 9 May 1915. In 1916 the goal was no longer to capture the ridge, but simply to pin down the German troops in Flanders and prevent them from being sent south to reinforce those defending the Somme.

An attack in Flanders had first been discussed a week into the great Somme offensive when Haig and General Headquarters were feeling optimistic about the way things were going. At that point the senior British commanders in the north had been asked to consider what large-scale attacks might be launched when the troops on the Somme moved forward. However, as early hopes of progress on the Somme faded,

left Aerial photograph showing shell craters in No-Man's land at its narrowest point between the German and Australian lines

The desolate battlefield of Fromelles on 11 November 1918

below Concrete blockhouses in the German outpost zone assaulted by the 14th Brigade *opposite* a ruined chimney at Delangre Farm. Thick barbed wire is obvious in both photographs over two years after the battle

directly into the gap between the two assaulting divisions. The Sugarloaf was located on the extreme edge of the British part of the attack; the Australians were intended to converge on it from the north once it was already under assault. However, if the British division failed to make progress, the German fire would then be able to cut across the paths of both divisions and probably bring the assault to a halt.

The two divisions selected to undertake the attack were quite different. The first, the 5th Australian Division, was drawn from across Australia, with the 14th Brigade from New South Wales, the 15th from Victoria and the 8th mostly from the less populated states. The 5th Division had been formed earlier in the year as part of the expansion of the Australian Imperial Force (AIF). After establishing itself and beginning its training in Egypt, the division had only begun to arrive in France at the beginning of the month and had taken over from the 4th Australian Division in Flanders between 10 and 12 July. Some individuals had gained experience of fighting at Gallipoli, but on the whole it was a very inexperienced unit and had only had the briefest of introductions to the rigours of the Western Front.

Alongside it, the British 61st Division was little better off. It hailed from the central English shires – Gloucestershire, Worcestershire, Warwickshire, Berkshire and Buckinghamshire – and, although it had been in France for longer than the 5th Australian Division, this was only by a matter of weeks. The 61st Division had arrived in the line in the middle of June 1916. Since then it had undertaken eight major raids and suffered steady casualties. As one of the later British divisions to be sent overseas, its original strength was already low and by mid-July there was a significant difference

between it and that of the 5th Australian Division. The British battalions had a front-line strength of only 550, whereas the Australian battalions were well over half as strong again. As a result, in the forthcoming attack, the British would only be able to go forward with one man for every metre of front being attacked, but the Australians would have three for the same distance. This difference went a long way to explain why, in the subsequent battle, Australian casualties were more than three times those of the British.

Haking's plan was to breach the German front line and then capture a second line believed to lie a short distance beyond it. The assault was to begin with a seven-hour bombardment both to cut the German barbed wire and soften up the strong points. The rate of fire would then intensify during the final three hours. At zero hour the

61st Division would attack south-west of the Sugarloaf, with its line stretching to just beyond the Wick Salient. Directly east of the Sugarloaf, the 5th Australian Division would attack along a line that reached as far as Cordonnerie Farm in the British lines and Delangre Farm in the German lines. It was on the eastern flank of the attack, between Cordonnerie and Delangre, that No Man's Land was narrowest and during the British attack in May 1915 a significant lodgement had been made by the assaulting troops at exactly this point. The fighting had been fierce and casualties heavy, with the remains of the British dead still lying between the lines. The Australians would be forced to advance over the remains of the British troops killed the year before.

The German line along this whole sector was held by the 6th Bavarian Reserve Division. It knew the area well, having held

it since before the 1915 British attack. The Germans had taken the lessons of that battle to heart. They had established deep and carefully laid out defences based on two lines spaced some distance apart. Their front line was made up of strong points consisting of machine guns built into and on top of concrete fortifications. Some machine guns aimed directly at the attacking troops; others sent plunging fire into the rear of the British lines. They were supported by other men in deep dugouts. Although the front line was relatively lightly held, it was backed by strong reserves in concrete blockhouses forming a network of mutually supporting positions. This created a deep outpost zone that protected further formal defences beyond. If an attack breached the German front line, it would be contained within the outpost zone without, hopefully, the second line ever being reached. Strong and carefully

controlled counter-attacks by the German reserves would then drive out any troops who had broken in. The outpost zone contained large tracts of almost untouched farmland, with intact buildings, pastures and long grass. It was complicated ground with which the Germans were intimately familiar, but which the British knew only from aerial and battlefield panorama photographs. From the higher ground of the Aubers Ridge, the Germans had excellent observation over all the British lines. Little could be done without the Germans knowing, and preparations for the assault in July 1916 were no exception.

In the days leading up to the battle, doubts grew among many senior commanders about whether the operation ought still to be carried out. Events on the Somme meant that GHQ no longer needed it, but Haig fell short of calling it off.

above Australian soldiers of the 53rd Battalion waiting to attack at Fromelles only a few minutes before the battle began

right Wounded Australian prisoners at a German dressing station on 20 July 1916 after the battle

right **German defences in the outpost zone attacked by the 31st Battalion. This was the expected second line that the Australians found so hard to consolidate**

The army commander responsible in Flanders also began to question whether it should take place. But he too failed to cancel it. The day before the intended start of the assault, which had been set for 17 July, wet weather blew in. Haking, however, remained confident and eager to continue with the attack. The date was simply postponed, first for 24 and then 48 hours. July 19 was fine and hazy. The artillery bombardment was ordered to begin at 11.00am, fixing the time of the assault as 6.00pm.

Although the number of shells fired during the seven-hour bombardment appeared high, its effect was limited. German aerial observers described the fire as being unfocussed 'like a scatter-gun'. Much of the German wire remained intact and the concrete strong-points and blockhouses were largely undamaged. The German artillery behind the front line was also able to fire unchecked, with little counter-battery fire having been undertaken. All in all, the Germans were still strongly in control of most of the battlefield when the infantry went forward.

Along the 61st Division's line, because of the low-lying ground and high water table, the British mostly attacked from behind tall breastworks, rather than from traditional, deep trenches. To launch their assault, the troops left their lines through a series of gaps, or sally-ports, in the breastworks rather than going forward in a long line. It was relatively easy for the Germans to concentrate their fire on these exit points and cause heavy casualties quickly as the troops were forced to bunch together. Once in No Man's Land, as the troops formed up into attacking lines, the German machine gunners enjoyed another fine opportunity to cause havoc.

For a short distance south-west of the Wick Salient, some of the Warwicks on the extreme British right managed to establish a lodgement in the German front line. But as the line swung north-east towards the stronger Sugarloaf, British casualties increased. The Gloucesters, Berkshires and Bucks were all largely cut down. Although a handful of men did make some progress towards the strongest part of the German line, it was to no avail. Facing the British line, the Sugarloaf remained intact, leaving the machine guns to cut down any movement in front. As a result, to the east of the Sugarloaf, as the line of attack curved round, the Australian brigade adjacent to the 61st Division suffered very heavily. These men from Victoria were also unable to penetrate the German wire around the strongpoint and overcome the lethal machine guns that brought them to a halt.

Along the Australian line, all the men went over the top in line, as opposed to exiting through sally-ports like the British. Away from the Sugarloaf, in the centre, the men from New South Wales rapidly tore into and through the German front line. Taking prisoners and two machine guns, they pushed on in search of the German second line. But this was not where they had been told it would be. Instead, the Australians found themselves caught in the German outpost zone. The absence of an immediate second line caused considerable confusion, and denied the men anything solid around which they could consolidate their initial gains.

On the left, the remaining brigade from Queensland, South Australia, Western Australia, and Victoria followed suit. They too burst through the German front line and began to establish new positions. All seemed to be going relatively well on the Australian centre and left. The fighting had been hard, but gains seemed to have been made, ironically, at exactly the same point that the British troops had pierced the German line just over a year before. However, the Australian advance formed the shape of a highly vulnerable arrowhead. Once the shock of the assault had abated, the German counter-attacks began and closed around the narrow point pierced by the arrowhead. Preceded by a heavy artillery bombardment, particularly in the Australian centre, pressure increased on all the captured positions. Australian reinforcements were sent over, but the situation deteriorated.

On the opposite flank of the line, the 61st Division at first intended to renew its assault on the Sugarloaf, where British gains were mistakenly believed to have been made. A new attack was set for 9.00pm. But at 8.20pm, once it was realised no British troops had reached the Sugarloaf, this was cancelled by Haking, and all British troops remaining in forward positions were withdrawn. To co-operate with the proposed British attack, some of the Victorians on the Australian right were also ordered to move again against the Sugarloaf. When the British attack was called off, word failed to reach the Australians and at 9.00pm they attacked alone with predictably disastrous consequences.

Throughout the night, in what was predominantly a very intense bombing attack, the Germans pushed hard against the Australian positions along the eastern flank of the attack. Beginning at around 3.15am, those Australians left in front of Delangre Farm were gradually pushed back across No Man's Land. In the centre, the New South Welshmen grimly retained their hold in the German line, but as dawn broke it became clear that any line of withdrawal would soon be cut. Behind the protection of a box barrage, these final men were withdrawn to the lines from which they had emerged the previous afternoon. It was a bitterly disappointing end to a fruitless battle.

The cost of the fighting had been high. The British 61st Division had suffered casualties of 79 officers and more than 1,400 men. The 5th Australian Division's losses had been more than three times as high. They had lost 178 officers and over 5,300 men, figures that corresponded very closely to the numbers lost by the British units that had attacked the same trenches the year before.

As had been the case in 1915, the battle in 1916 gained nothing. Orders found on the body of a British officer showed the Germans that it had just been a feint intended to pin down their reserves. They knew they had nothing to fear and began to prepare men to move south to the Somme. No lessons could be claimed from the battle, which many British and Australian soldiers at the time referred to not as Fromelles but Fleurbaix, and little else could be found to soothe the pain. Only Haking seems to have found some degree of consolation from what had occurred. On reflection, he noted, 'I think the attack, although it failed, has done both divisions a great deal of good.'

above **Dead Australian soldier in the outpost zone, photographed by the Germans after the battle**

Part II: The Missing

'A great number must still be in the ground and too deep to be located by ploughing or probing.' Major G. L. Phillips, Imperial War Graves Commission Australian Representative in France, 1927.

Overshadowed by the magnitude and cost of the Somme, the battle of Fromelles retains little resonance within Britain. Even in the south Midlands, from where most of the British casualties came, relatives are as likely to think their forefathers died on the Somme as in some largely forgotten corner of Flanders. In Australia it is different: Fromelles was the first battle fought by the AIF on the Western Front. The 5,300 men that Australia lost at Fromelles in less than 24 hours remains the most concentrated series of losses its army has suffered in any war or battle. In Australia, far from being forgotten, Fromelles remains a byword for the pain and incompetence of the fighting on the Western Front. People remember, and Fromelles is still a subject of abiding interest.

One of the people who remembered was Lambis Englezos, a school teacher from Victoria. His interest in Fromelles began in the late 1980s when he became perplexed by the appalling nature of the battle. In 1992 he helped to found The Friends of the 15th Brigade, the 5th Division's brigade drawn from Victoria. With other Friends, he got to know Victorian veterans of the First World War and Fromelles in particular. In 1996, on the battle's 80th anniversary, he made the first of many visits to France.

It was at V.C. Corner, just outside Fromelles, in 2002 that he first began to ask himself why so many Australian dead from the battle were unaccounted for. There are unknown soldiers buried the

above Lambis Englezos (left) at Fromelles in 2009 with Dr Louise Loe of Oxford Archaeology and David Richardson of the CWGC

below V.C. Corner Australian Cemetery Memorial, Fromelles

length and breadth of the Western Front. But something about the numbers at Fromelles struck Englezos.

V.C. Corner Cemetery is an anomaly on the Western Front. It holds the remains of 410 Australian soldiers found and interred after the war. When they were buried, it proved impossible to identify even a single body, so they were placed in graves but without individual headstones. Instead, two large crosses were set into the ground to honour the nameless dead. Overlooking the graves, a memorial wall recorded the initial 1,299 Australians missing presumed dead from the battle of 19-20 July 1916. Five of this number were later found and identified in the 1920s, reducing the number of Australian missing to 1,294.

Following his visit to V.C. Corner in 2002, Lambis Englezos began to question the idea that the remaining missing had

above **Rue-Petillon Military Cemetery, Fleurbaix in 1922 before the wartime crosses were replaced by headstones**

Were they buried some way from Fromelles, and so not included in the received number of unknown burials nearby? Some might have been, but surely not a significant number. If they had not been carried some distance away, were they still there, undiscovered, close to the place they had died?

Englezos began an energetic process of investigation. His zeal inspired others to join him: John Fielding, Ward Selby and Robin Corfield, author of a detailed account of the battle, *Don't forget me, cobber!* They became a formidable research team, scouring documentation and following any new lead they could find. Gradually they built up a picture that suggested the Germans had buried a number of Australian and British dead after the battle. Many, particularly on the left and centre of the Australian attack, had fallen in or very close to the German lines. For practical reasons, after the battle the Germans had removed as many as they could, or interred them quickly in battlefield graves. Englezos and his team found references to this in written accounts, including the regimental history published in 1923 by Generalmajor Julius Ritter von Braun of Bavarian Reserve Infantry Regiment 21 (RIR21), the German unit that defended the line opposite the Australians during the battle. There were photographs of dead being carried on light railway wagons. Aerial photographs, taken before and after the battle, showed that eight pits had been dug behind the battle front only days after the fighting. Of these, five were filled quickly with the dead of Fromelles.

A painstaking search was conducted through the Red Cross records in Australia that had been compiled to account for the missing after the war. Around 160 Australians were noted to have been buried by the Germans after Fromelles, with a

simply disappeared as a result of the battle. He established that, in addition to the 410 unknown burials at V.C. Corner, there were other large numbers of unknowns from the battle buried in cemeteries such as Rue-David (266) and Ration Farm (142), as well as smaller groups in other locations such as Rue-Petillon (22) and Y Farm (72). But even after taking those into account, something did not seem to add up. Englezos began to do the maths.

He knew that while some Australian casualties, through the fate of battle, would have completely disappeared, the number of unknowns should still approach the number of missing recorded on the memorial wall at V.C. Corner. Yet there was a significant difference. There were 1,131 unknown remains buried in the region of Fromelles; 1,294 remained on the memorial at V.C. Corner. Where were the missing men?

number of records specifically referring to burials behind Pheasant Wood. The eight mass graves visible in the aerial photographs were dug just behind this wood. The evidence suggested that a mass burial had been carried out by the Germans in the days following the battle. Had it been missed by the battlefield clearance teams after the war? Was it still there?

News of this hypothesis was first made public in 2003. Other parties became involved, supporting the work undertaken by Englezos and his colleagues. Chris Bryett, a Sydney lawyer, became enthused and was eventually moved to form a new association, Recovering Overseas Australia's Missing Inc. (ROAM). Public interest grew along with increasing political pressure on the government to take some kind of official action. If strong circumstantial evidence suggests that unrecovered remains might be those of Australian soldiers, the Australian army is obliged to investigate. The Australian Army History Unit (AHU), headed by Roger Lee, was told to look into the claims being made about Pheasant Wood. To do this, in June 2005 the AHU convened a panel of investigation in Canberra with a number of Australia's leading military historians, including Bill Gammage, Jeffrey Grey and Peter Stanley.

Lambis Englezos, supported by John Fielding and Ward Selby, presented his evidence. But the panel remained unconvinced. They knew from other sources that the battlefield clearance teams had been thorough, and they found it hard to believe a documented grave of this size would have been missed. They concluded the evidence was not yet strong enough to justify a more detailed investigation of the site. Englezos and his colleagues went back to work.

In July 2003 Englezos had met the British historian, Peter Barton, who was on a visit to Melbourne. Barton was co-secretary of the British parliamentary All Party War Graves and Battlefield Heritage Group chaired by Lord Faulkner of Worcester. Barton had stressed to Englezos that he believed the key to unlocking the mystery lay in the untapped resources of the Bavarian regimental archives in Munich. If any substantive new evidence was found to support Englezos's claims, Barton undertook to raise the matter with the War Graves and Battlefield Heritage Group to seek their support.

The AHU's panel of investigation also recommended exploring further the archive records held in Bavaria, as well as trying to find further documentary evidence from British and Australian sources. A request was sent via the German Embassy in Canberra for a search to be made for any files relating

right German photograph labelled 'Fallen English from the attack at Fromelles on 19.7.1916. The Germans saw no reason to differentiate between Australian and British in death

to Fromelles. It was a year before a reply was received, but it was worth the wait. In September 2006, Roger Lee received from Dr Lothar Saupe, curator of the Bavarian military archives, a copy of an original document written by von Braun, then a colonel commanding RIR21, that ordered the construction of mass graves for up to 400 *English* soldiers behind Pheasant Wood and laid out in detail the procedures for burying them. This document changed everything. As previously agreed, Lee set about reconvening the panel. At the same time, Peter Barton prepared to present both this new evidence and Lambis Englezos' original body of work to the War Graves and Battlefield Heritage Group and the CWGC. In December 2006 matters finally came to a head.

When the panel met again in Canberra, they were presented with the new evidence.

It was agreed that it now appeared burials had taken place at Pheasant Wood. But there was still no clear evidence to show that the remains had not already been recovered. The panel recommended a preliminary, non-invasive archaeological survey of the Pheasant Wood site using sophisticated geophysical techniques. Without actually undertaking a dig, the physical characteristics of the ground could be established to determine whether or not mass graves had been dug there and, if they had, whether they appeared to have been opened up again after the war. The aim was not to recover any remains, but to determine the probability of them still being there.

In London, Peter Barton laid out the situation to the War Graves and Battlefield Heritage Group. Aware that this important issue had previously been perceived solely as a matter of Australian interest, Barton also

did some maths of his own. The newly found German order required graves to hold up to 400 'English' dead. It would be impossible to estimate how many were eventually buried, but if it was true that around 160 missing Australians were unaccounted for, then surely any dead beyond this number buried at Pheasant Wood must be British? If 400 had been buried, then for every two dead Australians in the grave, it was possible there might be three British; this should no longer remain simply an Australian issue. Lord Faulkner, as Chairman of the Group, began to mobilise ministerial interest in Britain.

Englezos had already been in touch with Tony Pollard, Director of the Centre for Battlefield Archaeology at the University of Glasgow and a lecturer in Glasgow University's Archaeological Research Division (GUARD). Pollard was an acknowledged expert in First World War battlefield archaeology and had recently pioneered the use of a range of scientific processes to explore similar battlefield sites. In May 2007, the AHU commissioned a GUARD team led by Pollard to undertake a full geophysical survey of the Pheasant Wood site. At the same time Peter Barton was asked to undertake further archive research in Bavaria.

GUARD's survey confirmed that eight mass graves had been dug at Pheasant Wood. The metal scatter pattern suggested that these had not been disturbed since the fighting in 1918 had passed over them shortly before the end of the war. From two small objects found on the edge of the site a clear Australian link was established. The balance of probability had finally turned. Combined with the documentary evidence, it now appeared that the Germans had buried the dead from the battle behind Pheasant Wood and that the remains might still be there.

opposite An Australian Rising Sun collar badge uncovered at the Pheasant Wood site in 2008 by GUARD

right Relics of battle recorded by GUARD during the 2008 limited excavation of the site

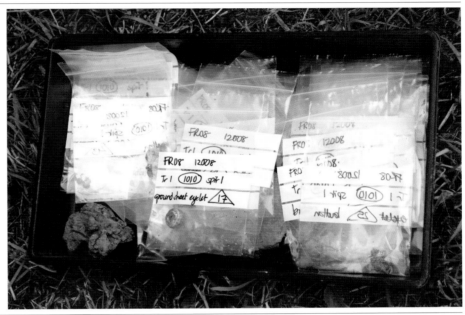

In May 2008, the AHU asked GUARD to conduct a second investigation. This time a limited excavation of the area was undertaken, cutting exploratory trenches across the surface of the mass graves. Nothing was removed; no remains were exhumed. The point of the exercise was simply to confirm once and for all whether a mass grave containing several hundred of the missing of Fromelles was still there. It was.

The results were extraordinary. There, for the first time in more than 90 years, the dead of the battle could be seen. Australian and British soldiers alike had all been buried by the Germans following the battle in 1916. Yet, in the immediate aftermath of the war, when so many others had been located and reburied within the dignity of an Imperial War Graves Commission cemetery, they had been overlooked. What had happened?

Documents in Australia confirmed that the Australian Graves Service had worked intensively in this area. But a report from 1925 acknowledged that along the Fromelles front line three years earlier there had still been 'many surface indication (sic) of very heavy death-toll and traces everywhere of bodies blown to pieces. A great number must still be in the ground and too deep to be located by ploughing or probing'. It is hard to say why the graves at Pheasant Wood were not found. Long grass perhaps made them difficult to see. They may simply have been overlooked. No definitive explanation has yet been offered. Answers might yet be found in Britain's National Archives, the National Archives of Australia, or the archives of the CWGC. For the moment, although 250 sets of remains have now been found and laid to rest in the new CWGC cemetery nearby, all we know is that the story is far from over.

Part II of this chapter is based on an article that first appeared in a special Fromelles issue of the Australian War Memorial's magazine, Wartime *(Issue 44, October 2008). Nigel Steel is grateful to the Council of the AWM for their permission to reproduce it here. He would also like to thank the historian Peter Barton for his help and detailed comments during the drafting of Part I.*

Uncovering the Fallen

Louise Loe

Oxford Archaeology is an independent organisation and a registered educational charity. It has four offices in England and two in France and employs around 400 staff. Within the Oxford office is a department called Heritage Burial Services, which is entirely dedicated to burial archaeology. Members of the team have excavated and studied burials - cremations and inhumations - from the Neolithic to the 20th century from all over England and in France. The excavation at Fromelles would be different however, since it was the first time since the burial parties of the 1920s had cleared the battlefields after the Great War that a large scale attempt to recover and identify soldiers had been undertaken. Dr Louise Loe tells the story of Fromelles from the archaeologist's perspective.

The Fromelles project represents the first time archaeologists have recovered casualties of the Great War on such a large scale. The type of work involved, however, was not wholly new to Oxford Archaeology. We had previously undertaken many excavations of large numbers of individuals: St Luke's post-medieval cemetery and crypt, London (1,053 individuals); the medieval and post-medieval burial ground at St Hilda's, South Shields (240 individuals); Lankhills Roman cemetery, Winchester (c. 300 individuals) and a Roman mass grave from Gloucester, being some examples.

The Roman mass grave was particularly interesting. It contained at least 91 individuals who were lying in no particular order, suggesting they had been buried in a hurry. Analysis of the remains revealed a mixed population of men, women and children. They showed no evidence of having been killed as a result of conflict. In fact, there was very little on their bones to suggest what had resulted in their sudden deaths and subsequent hurried group burial.

above The Oxford Archaeology team with colleagues from other specialist areas

opposite The back-breaking work of excavation by hand

This pointed to something that does not show on bones as the most likely cause of death. The best candidate for this was plague, possibly the Antonine plague (believed to have been either smallpox or measles) which is known to have raged through the Roman Empire in the first century AD, the probable date range assigned to the mass grave.

Although distanced in time and space from the First World War, the Roman mass grave presented a similar set of logistical challenges to those that we were to face in Fromelles. Like the bodies at Fromelles, the remains were buried in heavy clay which required skill to remove from around the bones and artefacts without disturbing or damaging them. Further, the matrix of remains was very complex – limbs overlapping limbs – so special recording strategies were developed to help interpret

above **The site showing the mass graves (under cover) in the background and the offices, laboratories and temporary mortuary in the foreground**

how the bones were positioned. This experience certainly stood us in good stead for Fromelles where similar conditions were encountered.

And this was not our only mass grave experience in 2009. Curiously, while we were slowly disentangling the bones of the Great War dead and carefully removing them from the rich loam of Flanders, another mass grave of young men was discovered in the white chalk of Dorset. This was completely unexpected. The grave was found during works to cut a bypass through the hills above Weymouth, as part of a wider scheme to improve transport links for the London 2012 Olympics. A large pit was uncovered, which contained some 51 decapitated skulls and skeletons, possibly those of Viking raiders. Like Fromelles, this discovery received wide international media coverage and caused great excitement.

Images of the grave, with the decapitated skulls and skeletons, were published and members of the public visited the site to see the remains for themselves.

The widely and openly publicised nature of the discovery threw into stark relief the highly sensitive nature of the work at Fromelles, where the public has not been allowed access to the graves and no images of human remains have been published. Being hundreds of years old, the possible Viking remains are distanced from our daily lives. In the case of the soldiers buried at Fromelles there is still a strong link to the present. In both Australia and the UK there are families waiting to discover whether their relatives will be among those who might possibly be identified amongst the remains. And if they are, those families will of course wish to commemorate them.

As soon as we were awarded the contract to carry out the work at Fromelles we began making plans in earnest for the excavation. There was a lot to organise in a short space of time. We had to confirm the team, purchase extra equipment, and set up a compound in Fromelles from which to operate.

To meet the unique requirements of this project, a team of around 30 specialists was assembled. It included a core group of traditional archaeologists from OA, including osteoarchaeologists (specialists in the study of human – especially skeletal – remains from archaeological sites), finds specialists and surveyors. We also needed forensic specialists, including mortuary managers, who came from Glasgow and Clyde NHS; a forensic radiographer from Basingstoke and North Hampshire Foundation Trust; a scene of crime officer from Gwent Police; a forensic photographer; and forensic archaeologists and anthropologists. Different members of the team had worked on mass graves in Bosnia, Guatemala and Iraq. Some had attended the scenes of mass fatalities including the Indian Ocean tsunami in 2004 and the 2005 London bombings.

The compound was set up around the site of the graves at the end of April 2009. It consisted of portacabins surrounded by a perimeter fence. There was 24-hour, seven-day-a-week security and strictly controlled gated entrance and exit protocols. During the project there was vast media interest and this system of controls was necessary to protect the site from DNA contamination and to offer high security and confidentiality; it also assisted with an effective work flow for the archaeological team and the management of communications, press and visitors.

Access was restricted to staff and the entire excavation area became a full 'PPE' (Personal Protective Equipment) zone, that is to say everyone who went onto the site had to wear protective suits, gloves, masks, hairnets and special shoes or overshoes.

The cabins served as changing rooms, a tool store and the survey data-processing suite adjacent to the recovery site. A few metres from here was the temporary mortuary facility for all post-excavation processes. Having the mortuary so close to the site was very beneficial, because it allowed everyone involved in the excavation and analysis to operate as one team, assuring the continuity that was so crucial to this project.

The mortuary was organised in a U-shape to reflect the workflow: remains were booked into a reception, from where they were taken for primary surveys in a radiography suite. Next was processing, an area set out for cleaning the remains. This was carried out by a team of up to six specialists, led by the mortuary manager. It was often here that some of the most revealing discoveries were made, such as an unused return train ticket from Fremantle to Perth, which was tucked inside a gas mask bag.

A drying area followed this, which led into anthropology and finds laboratories. Finally, when all analyses were complete, the remains were delivered to an environmentally-controlled store to await reburial. Additional cabins included offices and a press room for visitors and media.

Excavation of the graves commenced officially on 5 May 2009 and was marked by a formal ceremony attended by senior officials from the Australian and British governments, the CWGC, the village of Fromelles, and local people from the region. The first sod was turned ceremoniously, and then the site was handed over to OA.

below **Site map showing DNA protection areas**

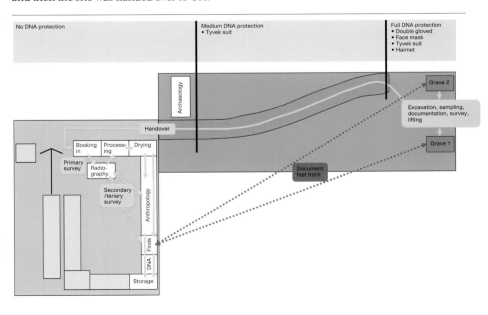

First, the graves were mechanically excavated under the close supervision of an officer for unexploded ordnance: even now there are shells and mortars from the First World War scattered across large areas of northern France and Belgium, and they can still be dangerous. Mechanical work stopped about 20cm above the top of the burials. They were then excavated by hand, two at a time, by teams of six osteoarchaeologists and one surveyor. Perimeter trenches were excavated, so that the graves were 'pedestalled'. For this operation, unlike traditional burial archaeology or investigations of modern mass graves for the collection of evidence for criminal trials, there was no archaeological reason to preserve and record the grave sides.

Osteoarchaeologists hand-excavated down to the artefacts and human remains (all skeletal), in stratigraphic sequence, that is to say in order of the highest, most recent deposits to the lowest, earliest deposits. For each grave and each layer of burials, we began with the trial trenches excavated by GUARD in 2008 and then worked outwards into the rest of the grave. It was essential that no artefacts or bones were missed, however small. The bodies had been buried in thick, sticky clay. This was a mixed blessing: overall, the movement of bones and artefacts in the ground following burial was minimal, but it meant that the best recovery technique – sieving – could not be employed. Alternative strategies had to be used and these included fingertip searching and metal detecting. We also took soil samples from key locations around and below each skeleton, and these were checked in the laboratory using digital x-radiography to look for any small bones or artefacts that could not be seen in the grave. Samples from different areas around the skeleton (for example, chest, arms and neck) were kept strictly separate so we would know where any items or bone fragments had come from. Samples of bone and teeth were also sent to LGC Forensics for DNA analysis to attempt to match them with DNA taken from living relatives.

We followed a standardised system for labelling every skeleton, artefact and DNA sample, whereby each was assigned a unique number from a running sequence, followed by the letter A for artefact, B for body (in this context used to apply to skeletons), or S for sample. Associations between the former two were recorded by survey, photography and written record. It was vitally important that any association made between an individual and an artefact was accurate, as this information could play a fundamental role in identification. A strict system was therefore employed in which associations

made by the excavator were checked and agreed with the grave supervisor. This was checked again by the photographer, who recorded the associations graphically, and the surveyors, who recorded the associations on a three-dimensional plan. A final check was made by the finds specialist when artefacts were recorded in the finds lab, to confirm that the location was consistent with its identification. A badge found by the feet, for example, was regarded as less closely associated with an individual than one found in the neck or shoulder region.

In many ways, this was a traditional archaeological project, based on the usual principles, employing the usual methods, and aiming to inform today's public about events in the past. However, unlike traditional archaeology where the focus is by and large on populations and what we can learn about how they lived and died, the focus here was on individual soldiers who died as a result of a terrible battle. Thus we prioritised evidence that might help with the identification of individuals, and took into account all the sensitivities of the living in a very personal way. It was crucial that the integrity of all the artefacts and human remains was maintained at all times. This was achieved by employing a working practice common to forensic operations called 'chain of custody'. Every transfer of a set of remains and artefacts from one section to another was recorded and signed. Strict observation of this protocol meant that at any moment any artefact or skeleton could be traced.

It took seventeen weeks to complete the excavation of the graves, yielding a total of 250 individuals with associated finds. Two of the pits (numbered 7 and 8) were found to contain no individuals and one, grave 6, contained the remains of only three men.

The other five held between 44 and 52 men each, the majority laid out north-south (across the graves) in two rows, one above the other, with a layer of soil in between. The graves were between just over 1m and just under 2m deep.

The anthropological and artefactual analyses undertaken by our teams were completed by 16 October 2009. Work stations were made for up to six anthropologists, who each examined one case at a time. Standard photographs of each skeleton were taken by overhead cameras and downloaded onto computers, along with the associated survey and finds data, the bespoke project database and digital x-rays. This real-time archaeological recording and analysis was invaluable in helping us to manage the information flow and to ensure the work was completed on time. It was, by any standards, a strict time schedule.

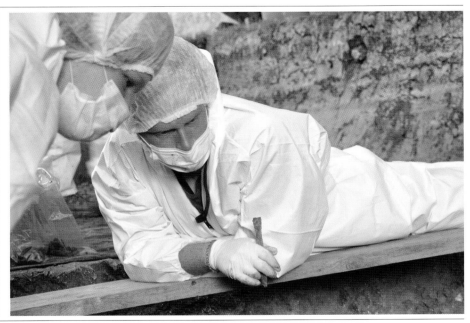

We found that all the skeletons were in a good or excellent condition. As expected, they exhibited extensive battlefield injuries (blast, projectile and sharp force traumas) – testimony to the horrors the men faced on the battlefield in 1916. In fact, the examples we saw at Fromelles have enormous potential to increase our understanding of skeletal trauma and this knowledge could be applied in the future to help solve modern forensic cases. There is currently very little research on battlefield trauma to the human skeleton in the published literature. Although there are numerous modern examples of such traumas, including those encountered as a result of atrocities, these rarely make it into the literature because of the legalities involved.

The age of the soldiers ranged from teens to forties, but most were in their early twenties. Details of physical characteristics such as height, facial features and build, as well as ante-mortem pathology and trauma (for example, healed fractures, longstanding infection or tooth decay), that is to say defining features that tell us something about the individuals before they died, were fully documented for the identification commission. Some historical records give eye-witness accounts of how individuals were killed on the battlefield, so we also recorded injuries that were sustained around the time of death. This includes injuries that may have caused their deaths, as well those that may have been sustained after they died but before they were recovered from the battlefield – unfortunately it is very difficult to differentiate between the two.

We were struck by the vast range of dental work we observed among the soldiers, including root fillings, dentures and crowns in a variety of forms (including solid gold). Unfortunately this is not as helpful for identification as it could be because the dental records to match them with do not exist – either they never did or they were destroyed during the Second World War.

Equally fascinating was the ante-mortem pathology and trauma evidence for disease and injury that they had before they enlisted with the army and which tell very interesting stories about their civilian lives. We saw, among other things, infections that probably arose in childhood; broken bones as a result of falls and interpersonal violence (subsequently healed); and osteoarthritis. Most interesting of all, however, was the high frequency and range of congenital defects (anomalies in their bones) which were acquired during development in the womb. These probably had little or no impact on their daily lives, but they are a fascinating indication of the often poor state of maternal health at the turn of the twentieth century.

The Germans who had buried the men at Fromelles in 1916 had been instructed to collect identity discs and personal effects to send back to the Red Cross and we expected to find only a limited range of artefacts. However, some 6,200 items were found: that is, about 25 pieces per man. They included pieces from military uniforms such as badges, buckles, buttons, fabric (including socks) and the occasional boot. All of these are very helpful in determining whether individuals were serving with the Australian or British Armies.

We also found traces of the soldiers' daily lives: the remains of medical kits, smoking apparatus, pens and indelible pencils. Among the latter were two gold-nibbed self-filling fountain pens, one made by Onoto, a British company that sells the same pens today. One of these was still in working order. There were also personal gifts, including crucifixes, given by the

above Use of metal detectors and other modern equipment helped to locate artefacts

opposite Janet Worthington, Robert McNeil, Caroline Barker (background) working in the temporary mortuary as part of the chain of custody

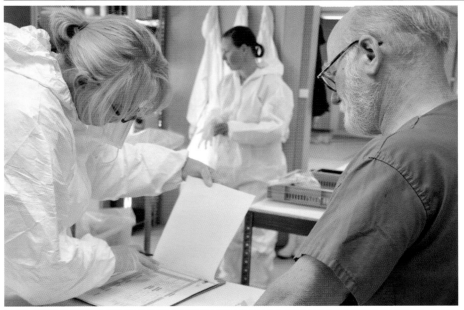

locals to the soldiers when they arrived in France. To our amazement, books, including bibles, had survived in the clay for over 90 years. One had passages clearly underlined. We also found a French/English phrase book, which included the expressions 'Bring me cigarettes', 'Do you speak English?' and 'Don't shoot'.

It is well known that soldiers made trench art from discarded shells and bits of metal or other material found lying about so it was no surprise to find rings and bracelets made from scrap metal. There were also purses containing coins. One contained two English coins, one Dutch guilder, two French francs, a 25-centime piece and eight Ottoman Turkish coins. Perhaps the purse belonged to one of the many Australian soldiers who had been at Gallipoli before coming to France. Our team meticulously cleaned, examined and recorded all these objects.

Items like these reveal the human side of the battle. Little keepsakes and memorabilia, perhaps exchanged with comrades or simply picked up, suggest that men were keen to hold onto something that would remind them of where they had been and what they had been through. Among the most poignant finds was the unused second-class return train ticket from Fremantle to Perth, mentioned above. Another precious personal item was a lock of hair in a leather heart. Such intimate reminders of the human cost of war are limited in the help they can provide in identifying individuals but they tell us a great deal about the young men who left home to fight.

Every artefact was conserved (short-term), photographed, researched and logged. At all stages, priority was given to the potential of the artefacts to assist with identification. For example, heavily corroded

items were radiographed to see if they carried important identification information, which helped prioritise them for subsequent treatment.

The group of artefacts associated with each individual was then analysed as a whole, looking at where the items were found in relation to the skeleton and what story they tell when put together. For example, a soldier wearing a British button, but with several items of Australian insignia, such as Rising Sun badges and shoulder titles, might have replaced a lost Australian button with a British one. Once this work was completed, the artefacts were then ready to be signed over to long-term storage where they, along with the human remains, were assigned their own designated space. Here, under full-time security, they were kept stable by maintaining a constant temperature.

We locked the doors to the mortuary for the last time on 16 October 2009 and made our way back to Oxford to begin our report on our findings. There was just a core group of us undertaking this part of the project. The rest of the team had moved on to work on new archaeology projects or gone back to their day jobs in the NHS, the police and other places.

Anyone visiting the site today will see that all of the graves have been filled in with earth and have been ploughed and re-seeded with grass. There is a great sense of calm about the place.

For all of us this project will remain a very special one – probably the most extraordinary project we will ever experience in our careers. To recover and examine the soldiers in a dignified and respectful manner, in order that they may be given their own burial in recognition of their sacrifice has been an absolute honour. Now, 250 soldiers, once lost, will be remembered.

The Finds and What They Tell Us

Kate Brady

The artefacts that were found with the soldiers buried in the mass graves at Pheasant Wood provide a unique insight not only into the era of the Great War but also into the lives of the individual soldiers who died at Fromelles. In this pictorial essay about the artefacts, Kate Brady, the team's Finds Specialist, asks what we can learn from them.

How telling are the items that a soldier carries with him into battle? This is the question that kept cropping up as we worked with the personal items we uncovered during the seventeen-week dig. There are many factors that would have dictated what these artefacts were: namely, military uniform design and the equipment issued for battle. But it became clear during the excavation and initial assessment of the artefacts, that some of these items were personal, had been selected by the soldiers to be carried into battle and therefore had meaning to those they belonged to. These items, in some cases in surprising ways, have enabled us to contribute significantly to the identification of individuals buried at Pheasant Wood.

Artefacts have their place in the identification process alongside anthropological analysis, DNA analysis, the study of ante-mortem records and historical research, but cannot be used alone, except in very rare cases, to provide an identity for an individual. The fact is, that artefacts are by definition portable. A button can be swapped and replaced, a lighter can be lent to a friend, a badge can be found and kept as a souvenir. An item a soldier had with him when he died tells a story, but it is not always an easy one to unravel.

The examples shown here were all found with individuals in the graves, and were therefore all with them when they were buried. This is just a small selection of the approximately 6,200 individual items that were recovered, cleaned, photographed, researched and recorded during the project.

opposite Pipe found in Grave 2

above Australian buckle with fabric from jacket belt

Boots

A small number of the soldiers were found wearing one, or occasionally both boots. Commonwealth soldiers' boots were desired by the German soldiers because they were more comfortable and practical than those issued by the German Army and therefore had been removed in most cases. It is likely that those still wearing boots had severe leg injuries, making boot removal either impossible or very unpleasant.

Although the British and Australian boots were distinctive in design, the use of boots to identify an individual as a member of the British or Australian Army is problematic.

Some Australian equipment was made in the UK, some in Australia, and designs varied between manufacturers within both countries. Australian soldiers could have been wearing either British-

or Australian-made boots. Further, a lost, damaged or uncomfortable boot could have been replaced with another.

Australian jacket belt buckle

These buckles are distinctive to the Australian uniform and were frequently found with individuals in the graves. They are approximately 55mm long and 25mm wide and made of brass. They varied slightly in shape, due to the fact that the Australian Army used several different suppliers for the manufacture of them. They were sewn to the fabric of the integral tunic belt, and therefore not easily removed from the uniform. This means that they are a particularly useful way to identify an individual as a soldier of the Australian Army, as it is highly unlikely that a soldier of the British Army would have been wearing an Australian jacket.

Buttons

Both the Australian and British Armies used distinctive buttons on their tunics/jackets. The Australian Army mainly used 'vegetable ivory' brown cellulose buttons on their tunics, with larger ones along the front and smaller on the pockets and epaulettes.

Other Australian buttons found at Pheasant Wood included the Australian Commonwealth Service button and the 'no borders' service buttons. The British First World War tunic was characterised by the presence of general service buttons, such as these found in the graves.

Large buttons were worn along the front of the British tunic, with smaller ones on the pockets and epaulettes.

The number and position of buttons found with an individual in the graves was an important factor when assessing potential to assist in identification. Buttons were (and still are) often swapped among soldiers or given to locals as souvenirs, and so a single button alone is insufficient evidence to indicate which army an individual fought for. Conversely, more buttons, found in the position they would have been worn on the jacket are a much more reliable indicator.

Many individuals were wearing braces, which were attached to the trousers by small metal buttons. Many of these buttons bore

the name of the manufacturers and are known as 'advertising buttons'. Examples include ones from Hordern and Sons' department store in Sydney, Australia, and ones from Hodgson and Morgan, Woolwich, London.

In other cases, makeshift braces attachments had been fashioned from re-used general service buttons.

In some cases, one or two British general service buttons were found with individuals who had several elements of the Australian uniform such as belt buckles and insignia, associated with them. This underlines the possibility that more portable items such as buttons were swapped between individuals or collected when found. Other examples of possibly collected items include a French artillery button bearing a flaming grenade symbol, and a flaming grenade collar badge, that would once have belonged to a grenadier or fusilier. Both of these items were found with individuals wearing Australian Army uniforms.

Iodine ampoule and safety pins

These small glass ampoules were carried by soldiers as part of the field dressing kit. They could be broken open when needed to apply to wounds. Several of these, still intact and still containing iodine, were found within the graves. They measured approximately 40mm in length.

Also part of the first aid kit were safety pins, used among other things for securing bandages. Several different types of safety pin were found with individuals at Pheasant Wood.

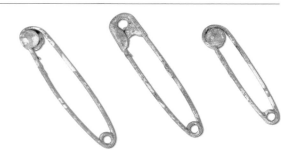

Toothbrushes

These were carried by the soldiers as part of
the 'holdall': a cloth roll which was used to carry
items of personal equipment and everyday
objects of use to the soldier. These included
a shaving brush, a cut-throat razor, cutlery,
a button cleaner and sundries such as bootlaces.
Soldiers were expected to mark their property
with their regimental number and regiment/
corps. However, none of the toothbrushes found
at Pheasant Wood were marked in this way.

'Australia' shoulder title

All soldiers of the Australian Army wore a
'flash' on each shoulder, bearing the word
'Australia'. Variations on this may have
included letters above denoting squadrons
within the Australian Army, such as 'MGS'
for Machine Gun Corps. Several examples
of these badges were found with individuals,
including some still attached to the fabric
of the epaulette.

Rising sun badge

Three Rising Sun badges were worn on the Australian uniform. One large badge was worn on the side of the slouch hat and one smaller on each lapel. The Australian soldiers would not have been wearing their slouch hats during the battle (photographs show that they were wearing 'brodie' helmets, so only two would have been present on the uniform during the battle). Where these badges were found with individuals, most had one: but occasionally two were present.

Trench art

Some items provide a fascinating insight into another aspect of life on the front. A few artefacts appear to have been made by the soldiers, perhaps as souvenirs to send home to loved ones and to pass the time. Two trench art rings were found with individuals. This was a common practice generally, and such rings were often made out of aluminium from the fuses of unexploded German shells.

The recovery of the metal was obviously a dangerous endeavour. Several examples of lengths of leather thong knotted and twisted into bracelets were also found.

What all the artefacts shown here demonstrate is that there is always a human story to tell. Sadly, given the time that has elapsed, many of these artefacts will have to be taken on face value and their stories never revealed, but they hint, nevertheless, at the hope and belief held by every soldier that he will survive to tell his tale.

Cigarette holder

This cigarette holder is made of silver, wood, and bone or ivory, in a wooden case. Inside the lid of the case a paper label, printed in gold reads 'H.M Silver. . .S', almost certainly the maker's name. This may have been the large and well-known silversmiths H. Matthews of Birmingham.

Coin purse and assorted coins

This leather coin purse was found with an individual in Grave 1. Within the purse were several compartments, each of which contained several coins. Due to the nature of the wet ground, over time these coins had corroded and become stuck together. Painstaking cleaning and removal of the concretions enabled the identification of most of the coins. The collection included eight Ottoman Turkish coins, probably brought back from Gallipoli, two French francs, one Dutch guilder and a British penny and halfpenny. Two other coins were too corroded to identify. We also found a small fragment of ribbed trouser fabric, typical of the thick cord of the Australian breeches. Although from the presence of the Ottoman Turkish coins it is possible that the individual had previously served at Gallipoli, it is equally possible that this was a collection that had been made as a hobby, swapping coins with other individuals. Again, the interpretation of the evidence is a complex issue and must be undertaken with caution.

Monkey charm

This charming little monkey was found in Grave 2 by a particularly delighted osteoarchaeologist. It measures approximately 20mm in height and has a small hole in the top of its head, probably where it was once fixed to a chain or pendant. The monkey is made of intricately carved ivory or resin. It is probable that this was a personal good luck charm or perhaps a souvenir from previous travels. Such items were not rare among soldiers but this was a delightful find and once again brought home the point that these men were so far from home and clung on to things that reminded them of safety and happiness.

Bible

This bible was found within the fill of
Grave 4. It was not close to any individual and
therefore we do not know who it had belonged
to. However, this extremely poignant item was
remarkably well preserved. The wet clay had
caused most of the thin pages to stick together,
but several passages on the visible pages had
been underlined and the margins annotated.

Heart-shaped pouch

This was one of the most moving artefacts I saw in the lab at Pheasant Wood. When this leather pouch was brought into the lab by one of the osteoarchaeologists it was immediately clear that there was something inside, and my immediate concern was how to open the pouch without damaging any evidence that might provide information about who it belonged to. With such items there is always a possibility that there might be paper inside, perhaps a letter or a photograph that might be invaluable for identification.

I carefully opened the pouch, which had been hand sewn round the sides and had a leather flap at the top, to keep the contents inside. Within the pouch was a copper alloy crucifix of the kind given to soldiers by locals on their arrival in France; a solid gold cross, more likely a personal possession; a thin fragment of glass stuck to a fragment of paper; and another tiny leather heart, hand stitched all the way around the edge. The glass fragment and tiny paper fragment bore no text or images and any other remains of whatever the item was had disappeared over time. After photographing the items together, I carefully unpicked the stitches around the tiny heart, to find that inside were the degraded remains of paper or cotton wool and a couple of tiny fragments of hair.

Train ticket

This tiny piece of paper was found folded up and with a PH hood gas mask. It was very wet when found and the two folded halves were stuck together. As it dried slightly it was possible to unfold the ticket and read the remarkably well preserved text printed on it. The text revealed that it was a return train ticket from Fremantle to Perth in Western Australia. It was made of thick paper, almost card, and was buff coloured, just like any train ticket one might have bought at any station. It was a poignant thought that this young man may have intended to use the other half of the ticket on his return journey. Fremantle and Perth are two of the places in Australia that enlistment took place and a number of soldiers who fought at Fromelles were known to have embarked at Fremantle.

Pens and pencils

A small number of fountain pens were found with individuals in the graves, one of which was complete and had a gold nib. Other fragments were from an Onoto pen, which are now high status, expensive items. Many of the soldiers had pencils with them, both lead, and purple indelible pencils which wrote in permanent pigment, useful in the wet weather and muddy trenches of the Western Front. Again, this is a reminder of what a vital link letters were with home. Millions of letters were written on the Western Front alone during the First World War and the Army recognised the importance of correspondence to the morale of the men, setting up its own postal service as part of the Royal Engineers in early 1913.

Lighter

This brass lighter was found with an individual in Grave 5. It was not immediately clear that this was a lighter, as it is fairly small and slim. We thought that perhaps it was a small case, possibly for a sewing kit. The case was corroded shut, so the on-site radiographer x-rayed it and it was identified as a petrol lighter. This is a good example of how modern methods helped us to interpret an object without having to resort to invasive techniques.

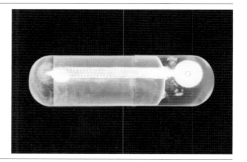

Pipes

Several well-preserved pipes were found with individuals in the graves, often in the chest area, suggesting that the pipe was kept in the top pocket when not in use. This pipe is made of wood, with a mouthpiece probably made of Bakelite or similar.

Phrase book

As paper has the potential to be an extremely valuable source of evidence for identification, it was always brought immediately to the finds lab for photography and examination before exposure to the air and light caused any text to fade or the paper itself to disintegrate. This small booklet was carefully cleaned in the lab, and the French text was translated by a French member of our team. It soon became clear that it was the remains of a 'Black Cat Phrasebook' which contained useful phrases for the soldiers on the Western Front to use when interacting with the French population. Phrases include 'Bring me some cigarettes and cigars', 'Do you speak English?' and 'Cut my hair quite short'.

Religious amulets

Several individuals were found with religious amulets of various kinds. These included crucifixes of various sizes, saints' medallions and rosaries. One crucifix was notable for its large size, measuring 90mm in length. It was also remarkably heavy, being made of iron with wooden inlays. The saints' medallions include a St Benedict medallion, and a St Stanislaus medallion.

The Scientific Overview and Identification

Margaret Cox

Science can work wonders, but only if it has the opportunity to do so.
Margaret Cox

When undertaking a scheme as complex as the Fromelles Project it is important that appropriate expertise is brought to bear on all aspects of the work involved. While the Fromelles Management Board (FMB) could rely upon the Commonwealth War Graves Commission to ensure the best possible specification and expertise for the design and construction of the cemetery, they agreed the need for outside experts to manage the scientific aspects of the work required to recover and identify the soldiers buried at Pheasant Wood.

Professor Margaret Cox has acted as a consultant to the Fromelles project, providing expert advice on archaeology and anthropology. A recognised world leader in the field of both traditional and forensic archaeology and anthropology, with almost 100 publications in this area, she is the lead editor and contributing author to the seminal work, The Scientific Excavation of Mass Graves, *published by Cambridge University Press in 2008. Margaret Cox has acted in a freelance capacity as forensic anthropologist to the Joint Compassionate and Casualty Centre at the Ministry of Defence over the last ten years. As such, she has regularly undertaken work for the MOD examining the remains of UK war dead from historic contexts world-wide. Margaret Cox writes about the challenges of identifying the soldiers buried at Pheasant Wood.*

When Oxford Archaeology began the fieldwork in May 2009, my role switched from project design and specification to one of quality assurance. It is normal in such projects to assess independently the quality of all work undertaken to ensure that it meets the requirements of the brief in terms of

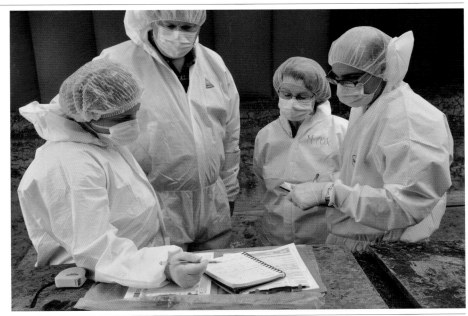

methodologies and standards. The period from October until December 2009 saw a further shift in role as I played a key part in the development of an appropriate identification framework for the project: one that met all existing guidelines such as those published by Interpol. No existing published protocols entirely suited the Fromelles Project, which was different enough from other previously undertaken mass grave excavations in its aims, objectives, the limitations imposed by time, and the type and condition of the evidence. The data collation and analysis process was undertaken in January and February 2010 and my role in this was as the chair of the Data Analysis Team (DAT); as a subject matter expert; and finally as advocate, making recommendations and presenting data to the Joint Identification Board (JIB) who met in March and May 2010.

opposite Caroline Barker, senior freelance anthropologist, examining finds in the anthropology laboratory

above Checking procedures for DNA sampling in the grave, June 2009. Left to right Ambika Flavel, Dr Peter Jones, Professor Margaret Cox and Dr Nicholas Marquez-Grant

above **The temporary mortuary facility at Fromelles**

Identification of the dead relies upon a combination of data sets. These are what we call 'ante-mortem data' and 'post-mortem data'. Ante-mortem data comprise what is known about the individual's life up to the point of death and post-mortem data is information retrieved about a person's life and death from their body, including artefacts. At the outset we had some ante-mortem data for most of the missing soldiers (*c.*1,650) and post-mortem data for the buried soldiers (250). The ante-mortem data varied enormously in quantity and quality. Most of the military records relating to UK soldiers from the First World War were destroyed during the Blitz, while those for the Australian soldiers survive and are extensive. Surprising as it may seem, we do not know the age at death of all of the UK soldiers, nor details such as stature, health, hair colour and weight. We have retrieved

photographs for some individuals, but some of these images are very small and/or poor in quality, whilst others are good and show facial features clearly.

The biological parameters of human identification (ID) obtainable from the skeleton are a mixture of those that are inherited and those that are acquired during life and at the point of death. Those that are inherited include DNA, genetic disease, eye and hair colour, and handedness. Those that are acquired are the result of life-style, circumstances, environment, and life choices. They include such factors as diet, occupation, living conditions, recreational activities, injuries and disease, medical interventions, and fashion. Clearly, where detailed and reliable medical and dental records, and family information and photographs (ante-mortem data) survive for missing people, this improves the possibility of arriving at positive identification. The greater the distance in time between the deaths of the unidentified and attempts to determine who they are, the less relevant information survives, and in some cases it may never have existed (e.g. medical records), or it may be unreliable. For Fromelles, challenges and restrictions were imposed by the condition of the bone, which varied from complete and intact to fragmentary; the paucity of ante-mortem records, particularly for the British soldiers; and concerns about accuracy of these where they do exist. We know for example that some men lied about their age at enlistment, and that this applied not only to younger individuals, but also to those who were over the specified age.

Further to this, it should be appreciated that although DNA is a very powerful tool, it may not be possible to recover both good quality Y STR and Mitochondrial DNA (see Chapter 5) from every one of the buried soldiers; informative family members may not exist or be traceable and, in some cases, they may not be willing to donate samples. For Fromelles, challenges imposed by all of the above are exacerbated by the fact that we have 250 skeletons and approximately 1,650 missing soldiers. Therefore, we potentially have 6.6 times more ante-mortem data sets (of varying amounts and reliability) than we do post-mortem data sets (of varying amounts and quality).

Clearly, biological evidence is more reliable and is more heavily weighted in the ID process than artefactual evidence. This reflects the fact that inscribed items such as personal effects that may be found with a skeleton may not necessarily have been the property of the soldier with whom they were recovered. They may be: but caution has to be applied and the exact position from which they were recovered in relation to the soldier's skeleton is important here.

There are two categories of identity relevant to this project:

1. Positive ID.
This occurs when unique ante- and post-mortem data types (for Fromelles – DNA only), are compared and match, providing clear and convincing evidence that suggests an ID is substantially more likely than not. Other biological evidence also has to be considered and must support this ID. If this contradicts the ante-mortem data for the individual under consideration, then issues of non-paternity and other irregularities have to be considered.

2. Presumptive ID.
This occurs where although no single factor alone justifies a positive ID, taken together the factors indicate that the suggested ID is substantially more likely than not to be correct. Such factors might include a number of skeletal indicators such as stature; age estimation; handedness; evidence (from enlistment records) of a known healed fracture; characteristics associated with ancestry; and/or a DNA match with a low probability level plus some artefactual evidence. DNA haplotypes[1] indicative of a particular and unusual geographical region or ancestry, may also be considered, especially in cases where the anthropology suggests a particular ancestral group may be present.

In the case of Fromelles the categories of ID applied and associated levels of proof are as described in Table 1 (overleaf).

For this project, our approach to the ID process is one that uses statistical analysis (e.g. nearest neighbour analysis); takes account of sampling bias; and is logical,

Category	Description	Level of proof
Category 1	Soldiers identified by name and consequently to Army.	Where there is clear and convincing evidence that suggests an ID is substantially more likely than not. This may include both positive and presumptive cases.
Category 2	Soldiers identified only by Army, or Army and Regiment / Battalion, and rank. This should not be conflated with nationality as men from the UK (and other countries) fought for the Australian Army.	Where sufficient evidence exists to assign an Army at the level of 'balance of probability'.
Category 3	Soldiers deemed to be of unknown identity.	Where insufficient evidence exists to place a soldier in a higher category.

above Table showing level of proof categories applied to the identification of soldiers recovered from Fromelles by the DAT and JIB

opposite Overview of the identification process used for the Fromelles project from 2010–2014

rigorous and repeatable. The DAT will collate all the available ante-mortem data for each of the missing soldiers from the Battle of Fromelles (c.1,650). They will also draw together all of the available post-mortem information for each of the 250 buried soldiers recovered from the graves at Fromelles. For the missing, these will be represented by ante-mortem data and for some, the DNA donated by family members.

The ID process will begin by assessing the DNA profiles obtained from the Y STR and/or mitochondria of the families of the missing soldiers against that of the buried soldiers. Where DNA is matched with high match probabilities, these cases will be examined first using a process of analysis that is designed to identify by name, as many of the buried as possible. These cases will then be subject to further assessment: looking at all evidence types (e.g. anthropology and artefacts) in the light of known ante-mortem data to see if they support the ID indicated by the DNA analysis. If they do, then a Category 1 ID (i.e. name) can be recommended for that individual. If the other data sets cast significant doubt upon the ID, the individual will then be considered for Category 2 or 3.

Following this, cases where there is a less convincing DNA result (lower match probabilities or multiple matches) will be considered. If other evidence sets do not support the tentative ID(s) suggested by the DNA then these cases will be attributed to either a Category 2 or 3 level. Where there is artefactual evidence suggesting a name or part of a name, these cases will be subject to further assessment by looking at all other evidence types to see if they support the ID suggested by the artefact. If they do then a Category 1 ID (i.e. name) can be recommended for that individual. If the other data sets cast reasonable doubt upon a possible ID, the individual will then be considered for Category 2 or 3.

Determination of a Category 2 level ID is likely to be based on artefactual evidence, such as army or regimental items. This will be considered in the light of contextual data (i.e. where on the body the item was located) to ensure, as far as is possible, that the item was a part of the soldier's uniform. Hence, items found in the region of pockets, which may have been transferred from the original owner, may be discounted as not being a strong enough indicator.

Once collation and analysis of all available data is complete, the DAT makes recommendations on levels and details of ID to the Joint Identification Board (JIB). This Board comprises two Board members representing the UK and Australian Governments, and it is they who will

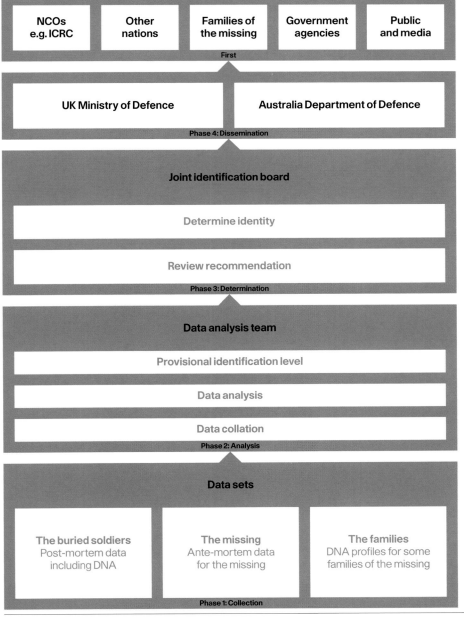

NCOs e.g. ICRC	Other nations	Families of the missing	Government agencies	Public and media

First

UK Ministry of Defence	Australia Department of Defence

Phase 4: Dissemination

Joint identification board

Determine identity

Review recommendation

Phase 3: Determination

Data analysis team

Provisional identification level

Data analysis

Data collation

Phase 2: Analysis

Data sets

The buried soldiers Post-mortem data including DNA	The missing Ante-mortem data for the missing	The families DNA profiles for some families of the missing

Phase 1: Collection

ultimately determine the identity of each case. This process will be repeated annually, from 2011 to 2014, where additional evidence becomes available for analysis and consideration. This allows a further four years for families of the missing to be located and encouraged to donate DNA samples. This will also allow time for further analysis where this is directed by the JIB.

In order to determine the identity of any of the buried soldiers, we need either a high DNA match probability and/or an associated artefact that suggests a name. In both types of case, all other surviving evidence must support that identity. Unless all of the families of the 250 soldiers buried in the mass graves at Fromelles come forward and donate a DNA sample, we are very unlikely to identify all of the buried soldiers. Science can work wonders, but only if it has the opportunity to do so. For this project that opportunity will be provided by the survival and extraction of good DNA from the bones and teeth of the soldiers, the survival of their genetic relatives, an appropriate DNA donor, and a willingness to participate.

Note

[1] A haplotype or haplogroup is a combination of variations that are inherited from one generation to another as a group. The combination of variations can be from geographically distinct regions. From Fromelles there is indirect evidence to suggest we might find evidence of Indigenous Australians, or those with Jewish or Romany ancestry.

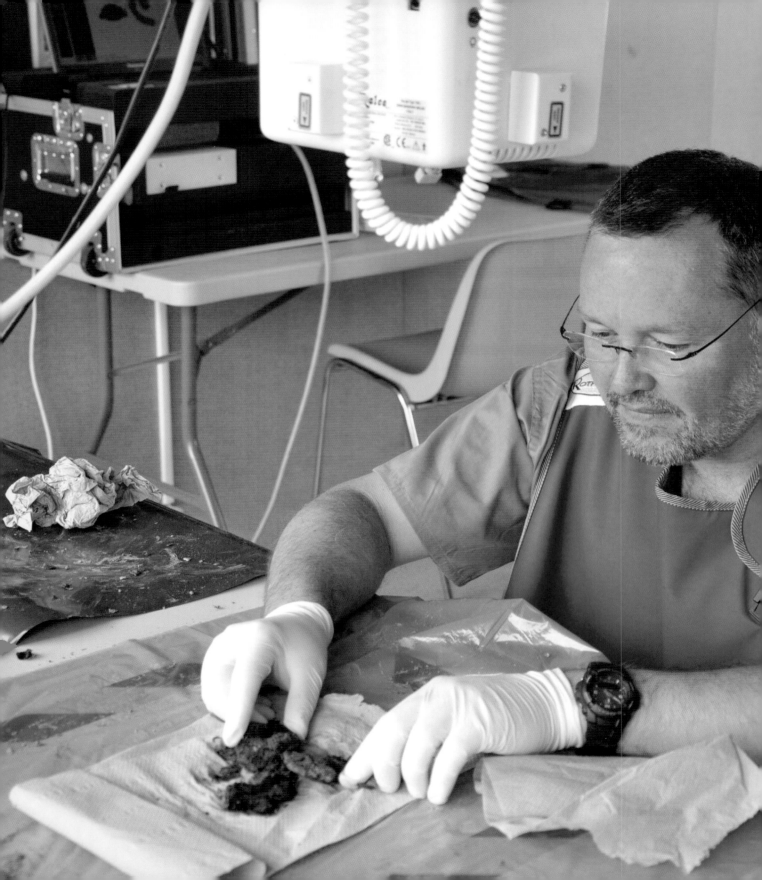

The Use of DNA Profiling

Peter Jones

DNA profiling is now a widely accepted process used for identification but its use in the Fromelles project is at the cutting edge of what is currently possible. Dr Peter Jones, a leading expert in the use of DNA Profiling and Molecular Genealogy, has played a key role in the Fromelles project. Here he talks to Julie Summers about the background and use of these scientific procedures in connection with the identification of men whose families have waited nearly a hundred years for news as to where they are buried.

Julie Summers: Can you give us a little background on DNA profiling and its current applications?

Peter Jones: Since its serendipitous discovery by Sir Alec Jeffreys at the University of Leicester in 1985, it has found many applications outside its initial use in human genetics. The most common use of DNA profiling is in associating an object with an individual's DNA found at a scene of crime. It provides an association that may warrant further investigation, as well as excluding the innocent. DNA profiling has also been used in paternity cases; in identifying contaminants in food stuffs; and in the identification of endangered species as part of CITES.

The current project, to profile human remains from a single site and then use this information and the DNA from living descendents to identify the fallen, is the single largest undertaking of its type to date given the time elapsed. DNA has been isolated from the remains of 250 soldiers recovered from Fromelles and has been compared to the DNA profiles of living relatives. Without living relatives it would not be possible to match a set of remains to a family group, as the DNA profile, without an external reference, is simply an anonymous

signature. Only with the DNA profiles of the relatives can an assignment of identity be made, but identification is only confirmed after all the evidence from the historical, archaeological and anthropological record has also been considered.

Julie Summers: What are the properties of DNA and how can they be used to identify an individual?

Peter Jones: DNA has some unique properties, in particular the way in which it is inherited from one generation to the next. Each cell within the body contains a nucleus. This is the central portion of the cell and within this are the chromosomes. These act both as a blueprint and as a structure, enabling cells to divide and propagate. There are 22 pairs of chromosomes in each cell, plus the sex chromosomes.

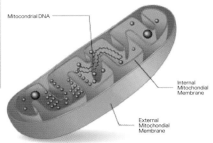

Mitocondrial DNA

Internal Mitochondial Membrane

External Mitochondial Membrane

opposite **Mark Farmer preparing objects found in the mass graves for x-ray**

above **Elements which contain DNA used for profiling showing the Y chromosome for male lineage and the mitochondrial chromosome for female lineage**

below **Structure of a DNA profile from chromosome to sequence**

opposite **Pattern of inheritance of the Y-STR and mitochondrial DNA showing potential paternal and maternal donors. Those on the direct male line are shown as blue boxes, while those on the maternal line are shown as pink boxes**

DYS388 (CEPH 1347-01) Example Sequence:

GAATTCATGTGAGTTAGCCGTTTAGCGAT ATATACATATTATGAAAC/ATT/ATT/ATT/ ATT/ATT/ATT/ATT/ATT/ATT/ATT/ATT/ ATT/ATT/TGAGACGGACTCTCGCTCTGT CGCCCAGGCTGGAGCGCAGTGGTGCGAT CTGGCTCACTAAAAGCTCCGCCTC

13 repeats 159 bp (ATT)13 Gene Diversity: 0.43561

They consist of a pair of X chromosomes in females and an X chromosome and a smaller Y chromosome in males.

The cell is divided up into specific subunits or organelles. These are visible under the microscope and in complex cells the organelle responsible for supplying the energy requirements of the cell is called the mitochondrion. The mitochondrion is essentially a cell within a cell and took up residence in complex cells about two billion years ago in a symbiotic relationship to provide the energy requirements of the cell in exchange for a stable environment. There are 200 to 2,000 mitochondria per cell depending upon its energy requirements. The mitochondrion has its own circular chromosome, separate from the main chromosomes, and is therefore present in greater quantities compared to the Y chromosomal DNA.

A DNA profile records the similarity or difference in the DNA sequence between each individual either as single base pair changes in the case of the mitochondrial sequence or the number of short tandem repeats (Y-STR) in the case of the Y profile. The change in DNA sequence is the equivalent of altering a single letter in a word or a sentence which may alter its meaning. For example, a simple typing error could replace the 'o' in 'for' with an 'a' to produce something quite different 'far'. It is also the equivalent of the accidental duplication or removal of words that can occur when cutting and pasting sections of text. The consequences of these alterations can be quite profound but in the case of DNA profiles, the effect is generally of no consequence. The DNA found at Fromelles is present in very low quantities and in a degraded form as a result of the passage of time but sufficient has survived to obtain a Y-STR and mitochondrial DNA profile from all 250 sets of remains.

Julie Summers: Can you explain more about DNA inheritance patterns?

Peter Jones: The basic rules for genetic inheritance were discovered by Gregor Mendel in the mid-nineteenth century, using sweet peas as a model organism. He is generally recognised as the father of modern genetics. In 1915, a year before the battle of Fromelles, the American geneticist Thomas Hunt Morgan demonstrated the inheritance of genes on chromosomes and the recombination of genetic traits through his work on the fruit fly.

Approximately half the DNA content of an individual is inherited maternally and half paternally. It is not an even mixing because the DNA undergoes reorganisation or

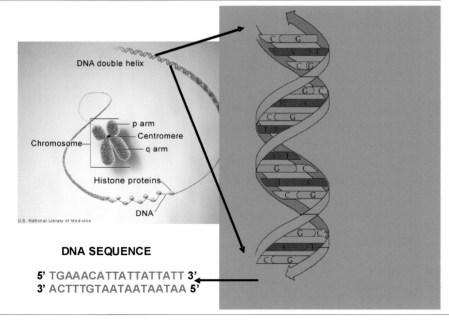

DNA double helix

Chromosome — p arm
— Centromere
q arm

Histone proteins

DNA

U.S. National Library of Medicine

DNA SEQUENCE

5' TGAAACATTATTATTATT 3'
3' ACTTTGTAATAATAATAA 5'

recombination. As a result, each individual has some traits that are predominately from the mother's genes and some traits that are predominately from the father's.

Establishing inheritance patterns between an individual and relatives separated by almost a hundred years and two or more generations is a much more challenging task. The standard chromosomal genetic markers used as part of the National DNA database are diluted and recombined through the generations, essentially rendering them of no practical use in identification over extended generations. This problem is overcome by looking at the inheritance pattern of those markers that are passed from one generation to the next and remain essentially unchanged or unshuffled, and therefore act as a baton in time. These markers are those on the Y chromosome (which determine male lineage), and the variation in mitochondrial DNA sequence (which determine female lineage). The DNA profile can be followed through the generations and lineage established.

Julie Summers: How does this work in the case of the soldiers at Fromelles?

Peter Jones: It is generally assumed that most soldiers were young, childless men. However, some of the older soldiers were fathers. If the soldier died without issue, lineage would need to be established through either his brother's male descendents, via the Y chromosome, or his sister's male and female descendents, via the mitochondrial DNA.

Females do not have a Y chromosome to pass on and males are not able to pass on the mitochondrial DNA. Both types of paternal and maternal lineage are shown

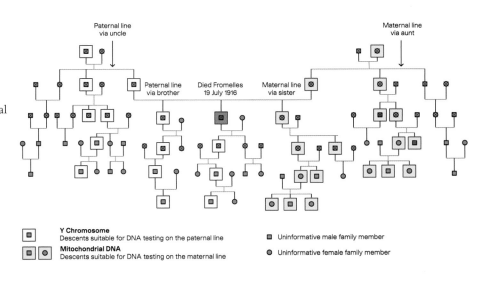

Y Chromosome
Descents suitable for DNA testing on the paternal line

Mitochondrial DNA
Descents suitable for DNA testing on the maternal line

Uninformative male family member

Uninformative female family member

in the diagram above. The lineage of the soldier is shown above and those individuals within the family tree who are on either the direct male line or direct female line are said to be informative and are shown as either blue (paternal) or pink (maternal) boxes.

When selecting individuals to provide a DNA sample for the Fromelles project only those informative individuals on either the direct male or the direct female line have been asked to be DNA donors. As the markers are essentially unchanged from one generation to another it is possible to include very distant relations to help establish a familial link. For instance, it is possible to go back several generations to find a common ancestor. This will identify a number of different branches of the family and then the line can be followed forward to the current generation. There are some

practical limitations with this technique but it is nevertheless very important in tracing distant relatives if no known informative family members are still alive.

Julie Summers: If the DNA cannot necessarily identify an individual, can it at least tell us where he was from?

Peter Jones: Human evolution started about 150,000 year ago in Africa and has steadily expanded to occupy most of the planet. Given the limitations on travel until recently, there were limited opportunities to form relations with distant populations. It is therefore not surprising that particular DNA profiles are common amongst certain ethnic groups or particular geographic regions. Particular DNA profiles, or haplotypes can be grouped together to form a haplogroup. From an individual's DNA

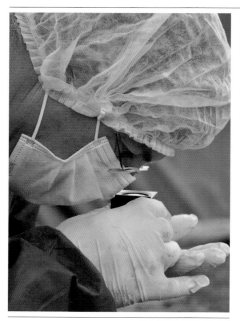

profile the haplogroup is obtained which may have a particular geographical origin or ethnic group.

This could be useful in the case of the Fromelles project. For example, it may be possible to determine if someone had Jewish or indigenous Australian ancestors within the family, as these haplogroups are quite specific. However, this technique is unreliable for assigning an identity; it only suggests a particular ancestry. It also does not determine how far back in time a particular genotype came into a family or indeed how it got there or under what circumstances.

The norm for individuals from the immigrant Australian population would be a European haplogroup but other haplogroups may be present. If someone is found with a unique genotype then this may give a clue to the person's identity in the absence of a family member coming forward to offer a DNA sample. It will not be enough to assign an identity but it is a good starting point for finding family members.

Julie Summers: How have you gone about searching for relatives and have they proved keen to get involved in the project?

Peter Jones: We have used a variety of techniques which included consulting lists of the fallen; making appeals in the media and organising roadshows to encourage relatives to come forward. Some families have been extremely resourceful, using genealogy websites or writing articles for local newspapers: approaches which have resulted in donors coming forward and sometimes discovering an entirely new set of relatives with a shared family history. Probably one of the most taxing tasks has been to look for relatives in cases where there are no surviving informative family

members. In these situations, the approach has been to scrutinise the family tree, trace all the branches for a common ancestor and then trace the progeny forward to the present day. This task has been greatly aided by on-line genealogical forums in the UK and Australia, as well as a band of enthusiastic genealogists.

All the families within the project without an informative line are encouraged to dig back as far as possible to find a line that has survived to the present day. For the paternal line this is made easier as the surname is passed on through male descendents. For the maternal line it is more complicated since the maiden names of all the female family members must be traced through the generations until the family of the soldier is reached.

Australian families have particular problems tracing distant relatives. Many Australian families are descended from British families with whom they have lost touch: indeed, a number of soldiers who fought for the Australian Army were born into UK families.

Julie Summers: How many people are we talking about?

Peter Jones: It is currently estimated that about 1,650 soldiers, British and Australian, are still missing from the battle of Fromelles. None has a named grave but all are commemorated on CWGC memorials. We know that 250 sets of remains from those missing were found in the graves at Pheasant Wood, so it might require all 1,650 families to come forward, ideally with a donor from both the paternal and maternal lines, to establish an identity. Interest in the project is substantial and about 50% of the families have come forward to enable the first set of identifications to take place.

Research conducted by the Australian Department of Defence, using records from the German Army and the Red Cross combined with their own archives, has produced a list of 191 names of men who are likely to have been buried at Fromelles. Unfortunately very few such records exist for the British soldiers as the archives were destroyed during the Second World War. The British side of the project therefore has to rely upon information provided by family members. Without the records we are more likely to achieve an identification of the UK soldiers if we have both the paternal and maternal DNA donors.

Julie Summers: Are you using clues other than DNA in your attempts to identify the men found at Fromelles?

Peter Jones: Yes, we cannot rely on DNA alone as there will be occasions when the profiles are not unique. As well as the records in the Australian archives, artefacts found in the mass graves will form part of the overall identification process. The German forces were very diligent in removing personal artefacts from the bodies so they could be returned to soldiers' families. They were also ordered to remove the dog tags, if present, and these too were returned to the families, via the Red Cross, in 1917. Additional clues come from descriptions in the military records of how a soldier was killed or even about injuries he had before joining up. It is possible to use such information to confirm identity.

However, it is not possible to use this information alone to assign an identity. At best it can identify an army or possibly a unit but not an individual unless a specific named object is found associated with a set of remains. Even then, this type of evidence must be considered with care as association does not always confer identification.

Although the use of DNA is powerful it may not be possible to locate the informative relatives. So far 94 identifications have been achieved in the first year of the project, all of which have been identified as part of the Australian army. These IDs have been generally the result of DNA data providing strong evidence that points towards an individual. The combination of circumstantial data such as personal items and artefacts along with anthropological data and historical accounts were all examined in conjunction with the DNA data. At least three out of five of these data sets were required when determining an ID. The identification of an individual was decided when there was clear and convincing evidence that indicated an ID was substantially more likely than not.

Where there was doubt or inconclusive data then an ID was not confirmed.

To date, no British soldiers have been personally identified out of the three British and 42 unknowns that exist. The lack of identified British soldiers could be explained in a number of ways. They may not have been recovered by the Germans at Pheasant Wood, as they were fighting to the west of the Australians; we may not have the families of the British soldiers; or we may have only one side of the family and therefore an inconclusive result. We are heavily reliant upon DNA donors from both the maternal and paternal side to initiate the identification process. Over the period 2010 to 2014, British and Australian families will be able to conduct further genealogical research to identify informative DNA donors to enable their profiles to be searched against the outstanding156 sets of remains.

A New Cemetery for a New Century

Julie Summers

Following the discovery of the remains of servicemen from the Battle of Fromelles, the Commission had to decide how to approach the whole question of designing a brand new cemetery to accommodate up to 400 graves that were believed to be necessary. A whole team was needed to realise the project, covering almost every department in the organisation. For this chapter, Julie Summers interviewed three members of the team who offered an overview of the challenges posed by the construction of the new cemetery at Fromelles and also in an attempt to place the work in the historical context of the Commission's other cemeteries.

Architect Barry Edwards has worked at the Commonwealth War Graves Commission since 1995. Much of his work to date has involved the maintenance of the existing buildings, cemeteries and memorials that were constructed in the aftermath of the two World Wars. Even today the necessity for new structures and memorials requires the work of an architect and Barry has been involved in several projects including a new memorial to Chinese casualties in Hong Kong and memorials to the Indian troops of the First World War in the Middle East. This included the extension of existing memorials in locations such as Abyssinia, Ismalia, Manara and Suez in Egypt and Beersheba, Deir el Belah, Haifa and Jerusalem in Israel. It has also included the reconstruction, from masonry fragments and photographs, of the entrance to the reinstated Zehrensdorf cemetery in a former Russian occupied sector of Berlin.

David Richardson, the Fromelles Project Manager, has been based at the Commission's French Headquarters at Arras since 2005 and has worked as a horticulturist with the CWGC since 1987. David has

opposite Cross of Sacrifice at Fromelles (Pheasant Wood) Cemetery

below The cemetery site at Fromelles prior to work commencing in 2009

grounds of access and water-logging. The ground near Pheasant Wood is very boggy and the site may have posed some access difficulties for visitors. A second site was rejected for similar reasons but the third site, the one where the cemetery now stands, is elevated so it has good views, and is on a slope which it was hoped would encourage drainage and water run-off. It is an excellent location from an historical point of view as it overlooks the scene of the battle to the north. From the Cross of Sacrifice terrace V.C. Corner Australian Cemetery Memorial can be seen about 1.5km away and of course V.C. Corner has enormous resonance for Australians so the link is both poignant and significant.

Julie Summers: You have talked about the challenges presented by the current site in Fromelles. How does that differ from what the architects of the 1920s encountered?

David Richardson: One major challenge at Fromelles has been the ground. It is heavy clay and a geological survey flagged up the problems of drainage that we would face and also alerted us to the fact that everything would have to be underpinned by piles driven into the ground. The trouble with clay is that it is an unstable base. In the summer it dries out and shrinks, in the winter it becomes waterlogged and swells. Houses built on clay are susceptible to subsidence and cracking. Clearly we did not want to introduce the potential for damage from the outset so everything is pile-driven to a depth of at least 5m – the cemetery walls, the terrace, the entrance, the Cross of Sacrifice and the headstone beams. Drainage was the other big issue. We wanted to ensure that the site would not get waterlogged in the winter but we also wanted to be responsible towards

worked all over the world and has an affinity with the Australians since living and working on the Gallipoli Peninsula in the 1990s for two and a half years. After working as a horticultural manager in the UK and later in the Middle East, Africa and extensively in Asia and the Pacific regions, David was appointed as the Fromelles project manager in September 2008. He has seen the project from its earliest planning stages through to the completion of the first new CWGC cemetery in over 50 years.

Brian Davidson joined the Commission in 1983 and has worked in many structural capacities. He is currently both the Director of Works and Director of Technical Services, leading on matters of horticulture, Works and IT. Over the years he has been involved in the reconstruction of the cemeteries in Lebanon following the civil war, the reconstruction of the Hargeisa War

Cemetery in Somaliland following internal strife between Northern Somalia and the Mogadishu war lords; and in Iraq in maintaining and planning reconstruction of the cemeteries following the first Gulf War. He is also the 'Technical Lead' on a number of other structural projects including the major renovation of the Helles Memorial on the Gallipoli Peninsula in Turkey.

Julie Summers: Was the site of the cemetery at Fromelles already selected by the time you arrived in France or did you have a choice of potential sites?

Brian Davidson: There were several sites that were considered as possible locations for the new cemetery. The first option, of course, was to use the low-lying land where the remains had been interred for the last 93 years but we soon dismissed this on the

our neighbours so we have included a collecting tank that will hold the excess water gathered from the drains and this water will be diverted down to the local stream rather than running into the gardens of the neighbouring houses. We also had to think about disabled access. That was not an issue in the immediate post-war era, although of course a very large number of men from the First World War lost limbs and so would have found visiting certain sites difficult. Many Commission memorials and terraces have steps, as does ours, but we have also included ramps so that everyone can have access to the Cross of Sacrifice terrace.

One of the other major challenges has been working to a very tight timetable. At the outset it was agreed that the new cemetery would open on the anniversary of the battle of Fromelles in 2010 and therefore the process of agreeing a site, acquiring the

land through the French Government, using the Commission's special status within the War Graves Agreement, and then actually carrying out the whole construction process has added a huge degree of time sensitivity. Burials at the site began on 30 January 2010 and because we were burying 250 casualties we had to modify the cemetery construction to allow for such a large-scale burial. This meant that the cemetery had no topsoil until all the burials were completed and we began the horticultural phase of the project. Turf, roses and border plants were all grown in local nurseries for the project and our gardening teams worked hard to ensure that the site was completed in time for the July dedication. The timescale was tight for allowing the plants to establish and despite our expertise we were to some extent at the mercy of the weather. The finished cemetery was always planned to be no different from

opposite Aerial shot shows how well the design of the cemetery reflects the site in the village of Fromelles

above Construction of the cemetery during September 2009

right By the end of September the walls were in place and the cross terrace well underway

related to soldiers buried at Pheasant Wood. Although the Joint Identification Board did not convene until March 2010, after the burials, families, were reassured throughout that everything possible was being done to identify these men. Many of our cemeteries worldwide have un-named headstones and the tens of thousands of names on our memorials commemorate those with no known grave. I feel that we will have achieved our aim of giving each of these men an individual burial and if we can name any individuals that will be an enormous bonus.

Julie Summers: You have indicated that a great deal of preliminary work and experimentation was necessary.

Brian Davidson: This is an interesting point. We had the unusual situation here where the burials and the cemetery construction were

---

those which are already found in the region and on completion the brick and stone features, the planting and the headstone borders all look very familiar. Much of the engineering and the application of new technology is hidden below the surface.

Julie Summers: You have been working closely with the experts from Oxford Archaeology. Can you tell us what your impressions have been from this collaboration?

David Richardson: Being based at Fromelles for the duration of the project I have had a unique opportunity to work closely with the team from Oxford Archaeology, as well as the consultant experts Professor Margaret Cox and Dr Peter Jones. I had no previous experience of an archaeological excavation and it was a great opportunity to observe the team and learn. I was apprehensive about

seeing the actual graves and found them very moving but I was constantly struck by the dedication of the team from O.A. – they had an incredibly wide range of experience and I was constantly fascinated by the precision and skill they brought to the project. As a very diverse group we were able to develop into a tight-knit and close team; this was important as the excavation was in the public eye and it was essential that it was a success. The excavation was delivered on time and to the highest level of excellence – visiting archaeologists from France and the UK commented on the high standard of work that was being undertaken. The excavation developed from a mass grave with an unknown number of casualties to individuals still un-named but each with unique characteristics and, in the main, associated artefacts. I was particularly moved when I met people who believed that they were

above **Construction of the schist, burial layer and sarcophagi in preparation for the funerals that would take place in February**

opposite above **Finishing of the base of the cross is done by hand at the workshop in France as it would have been in the 1920s**

opposite below **Forceville Communal Cemetery and Extension, France, designed by Sir Reginald Blomfield**

happening at the same time, which meant that we had to take the ceremonial aspects into consideration at the early design phase. We therefore constructed a trial burial area at our operational centre in Arras to replicate the burial conditions. We prepared a gravel base on which we placed preformed sarcophagi and encased each with a gravel infill. This not only provided support for the 250 individual burials, but also supplied drainage: an important asset for the future maintenance of the cemetery in an area where heavy clay is the predominant soil. This trial was successful and has been replicated in the cemetery.

Julie Summers: How much was done by way of experimentation in the past?

Barry Edwards: In the 1920s, work was proceeding at such a pace that it might seem

there was little time for research and experimentation, but that would be to do an injustice to the architects, engineers, horticulturalists and artists who worked for the Commission in the early days. We know, for example, that three experimental cemeteries were constructed by 1920 – two on the Somme at Louvencourt and Forceville and a third at Le Tréport near Dieppe. They were all designed by Sir Reginald Blomfield. The cemetery at Forceville was deemed to be the most successful, judged not only on its design and layout but also on a cost basis. This valuable experiment allowed a budget for the construction of cemeteries to be drawn up which, out of interest, they calculated to be £10 per grave, with the understanding that this was a sliding scale as smaller cemeteries would be more expensive and larger ones less so, per grave. In fact, almost everything they did had to be

designed from scratch. The lettering for the headstones was the subject of lengthy discussions. The inscriptions had to be read at a 45° angle so that someone scanning the lines of headstones or looking from a standing position would be able to read the names. Similarly, there was concern when designing the memorials that the lettering should be visible from below, so slabs of stone were erected high up on scaffolds at the Commission's Headquarters in Baker Street so experiments could be conducted. I think it would be fair to say that the Commissioners were keen to leave as little as possible to chance. And that is still the case today.

Julie Summers: How did they overcome the problems of subsidence and drainage in the early days?

Brian Davidson: In the 1920s the architects did not have much flexibility when it came to choosing sites. By and large land was close to existing cemeteries or given to the Graves Concentration Units by the government with little or no consultation with the principal architects. Do not forget that in the 1920s the architects were designing many of their cemeteries around already existing burial sites. In the main, graves concentration and registration, carried out by the army, had to be completed before cemetery construction could begin. Other cemeteries had been started close to field hospitals during the war, such as Etaples Military Cemetery in the Pas de Calais and Lissenjthoek near Ieper. In those cases the architects had to make do with the sites they were given. Despite this, the cemeteries and memorials were designed and built to the highest standards using the best materials to ensure permanence. That is not to say that occasional problems of subsidence and drainage has not occurred; some of our sites in Italy for instance are located on steep inclines or in seismically active areas and this has required work to strengthen the foundations.

With regard to drainage, there was not usually a problem if the soil was permeable. A number of low lying sites, or those constructed on impermeable soil however sometimes suffer from the effects of seasonal flooding.

Julie Summers: This new cemetery comes out of the tradition of Commission cemeteries from the 1920s. What can you tell us about how the Commission's architects worked at that time?

Barry Edwards: The Commission was set up in May 1917 and one of the first appointments was that of Sir Frederic Kenyon whose official role was to act as artistic adviser. Publicly, he was to give vision to the Commissioners' ideas for the cemeteries and memorials. Privately, Fabian Ware, the founder of the Commission, was anxious for Kenyon to intervene before differences of opinion between the three principal architects could be voiced in the open. The three architects were Sir Edwin Lutyens, Sir Reginald Blomfield and Sir Herbert Baker. They all had views on how the dead should be commemorated and it led to some heated discussions, particularly between Lutyens and Baker, who had already had a very public dispute over work in Delhi before the war. These three architects oversaw the designs by junior architects for all the cemeteries in France and Belgium. These included Charles Holden, who later became a Principal Architect; the South African Wilhelm Clement von Berg; W. H. Cowlishaw and N. A. Rew. They worked at a colossal pace and had considerable freedom in the interpretation of their individual cemeteries, although certain features, such as the uniform headstones, the Cross of Sacrifice and the Stone of Remembrance (for 1000+ headstones) were normally incorporated. It is still possible to distinguish the individual architect's style in design, use of materials and, above all, use of imagery and architectural features. The pace of construction in France and Belgium during the 1920s was extraordinary. Cemeteries sprang up at a great rate and by the mid-1930s over 970 architecturally constructed cemeteries had been dedicated in France and Belgium alone. Construction in Italy was completed first, with 19 cemeteries containing 4,000 burials finished by the mid-1920s, and in Gallipoli the 38 cemeteries were well underway by the same period.

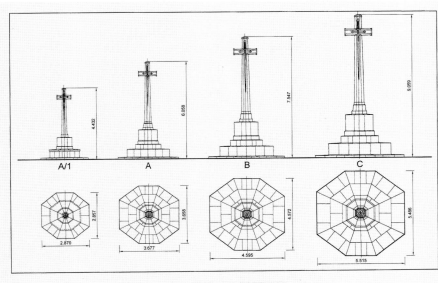

THE CROSS OF SACRIFICE

A/1   A   B   C

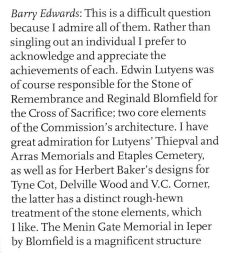

opposite clockwise from top left Newly quarried blocks of Portland Stone; blocks hewn and prepared for slicing into headstones; blank headstones awaiting inscriptions; inscribing headstones

above Blomfield's scaled Crosses of Sacrifice for different sizes of cemetery

below Installation at Fromelles of the base for the Size A Cross of Sacrifice

Julie Summers: *Which of the Commission's original Principal Architects do you most admire?*

Barry Edwards: This is a difficult question because I admire all of them. Rather than singling out an individual I prefer to acknowledge and appreciate the achievements of each. Edwin Lutyens was of course responsible for the Stone of Remembrance and Reginald Blomfield for the Cross of Sacrifice; two core elements of the Commission's architecture. I have great admiration for Lutyens' Thiepval and Arras Memorials and Etaples Cemetery, as well as for Herbert Baker's designs for Tyne Cot, Delville Wood and V.C. Corner, the latter has a distinct rough-hewn treatment of the stone elements, which I like. The Menin Gate Memorial in Ieper by Blomfield is a magnificent structure

which retains a high public profile with its nightly Last Post ceremony.

What is clear is that each of them interpreted Kenyon's artistic vision of an English country churchyard in his own way and this gives the Commission's cemeteries their real character. They conform to a basic pattern but each is an expression of the architect's ideas. Although not among the original principal architects, I also much admire the work of Philip Hepworth (in France, Holland and Germany) and Louis de Soissons (Italy) who designed cemeteries and memorials following the Second World War.

Julie Summers: *What influenced the choice of materials for the new cemetery?*

Brian Davidson: A great many of the First World War Commission cemeteries in France utilise the pleasing combination of thin (Boom) bricks with white limestone trimmings. The distinctive appearance this creates immediately brings to mind the work of the Commission and this also set the template for the new cemetery at Fromelles. Nearby examples of this style can be seen at Rue Petillon, Rue du Bois and Aubers Ridge Cemeteries. Some other cemeteries in the immediate area utilise irregular coursed stone that we call *Gres de Poulser* in lieu of Boom Bricks. This material can be seen at V.C. Corner, Le Trou Aid Post and Anzac Cemeteries. These three cemeteries were all designed by Herbert Baker so the use of this material became closely associated with this architect.

The headstones are made from Portland Stone, a noble material, used for this purpose by the Commission in the majority of its cemeteries across the world. The Type A Cross, the terrace, the wall copings and stone trimmings of the entrance building are of

Massangies Roche Jaune Claire, a durable French limestone again common in Commission cemeteries. There are in fact some 30 types of stone and marble used by the Commission throughout the world but on the Western Front Portland Stone is predominant.

Julie Summers: Why does this cemetery have a Cross of Sacrifice but no Stone of Remembrance?

Barry Edwards: This is because Blomfield designed four different sizes of cross so that even the smaller cemeteries could have one. The Type A Cross is the third largest, standing over 6m high. The largest size, such as you would see at Tyne Cot, our biggest cemetery in the world, is just over 9m tall. Lutyens, however, did not wish his stone to be scaled down. He was very precise about its dimensions and felt that reducing its size

would dramatically affect the impact it had. As a rule of thumb, only cemeteries with over 1000 burials have a Stone of Remembrance, though of course there are exceptions to this rule. By comparison, all but the smallest cemeteries have a Cross of Sacrifice.

Julie Summers: Tell me about how the design for the cemetery was influenced by the landscape and landmarks around it?

Barry Edwards: The battle of Fromelles was fought over a period of two days and it was a bloody and concentrated affair. The church tower, which is clearly visible from the cemetery, was used by the Germans as a lookout post. V.C. Corner, the Australian cemetery and memorial, lies just 1.5km from the site of Fromelles Cemetery, so that the new site fits well into the historical landscape. The shape of the cemetery grew organically to

some extent. One section of the plot's boundary was cut off at an angle and it seemed to me to make sense to reflect this in the cemetery outline, which is why we have ended up with the rather pleasing shape of a hexagon. The splayed angles encourage focus on a central point and this meant that the headstones could be set to face southwards towards the cross. This of course means that the headstones potentially get sun on them for most of the day which makes reading the inscriptions somewhat easier. It also helps with planting as the shrubs and roses are on the south side and not in the shade of the headstone.

Julie Summers: How much involvement have you had in the horticultural design of the cemetery?

Barry Edwards: The horticultural design represents a significant component of the overall cemetery design; the two aspects need to be considered together to ensure that they both contribute to the same objective. I spent a long time talking to my colleagues in the Horticultural Department about the planting for this cemetery. I knew, for example, that although I wanted symmetrically balanced trees behind the cemetery partially to protect the adjoining properties, I did not want any trees to grow directly behind the Cross and obscure its clearly defined profile. Likewise, I did not want to see trees in positions within the cemetery that would obscure the view from the Cross towards V.C. Corner. On the other hand, I included two niches in the northern walls so that planting could be introduced to provide colourful focal points at the ends of the side avenues when seen from the terrace at the top of the cemetery. There will also be planting between the double walls in the terrace and alongside the ramps

leading up to it. It was always the case that the architects and horticultural experts worked in close collaboration during the construction of a cemetery. This is important, because it is through the coordinated vision of the architect and the landscapers that the cemetery achieves its character. Kenyon made it clear in his report in 1918 that the particular character of the cemeteries would be best achieved by recreating the characteristics of an English churchyard. One interesting point at Fromelles, which I do not think has happened elsewhere, is that the level of the cemetery will be raised after the burials have taken place. This is because cemetery construction and burials are being undertaken simultaneously rather than sequentially, as would have happened in the 1920s. One hundred, 40-ton lorries will deliver sufficient topsoil to cover the cemetery and provide sufficient depth for planting.

Julie Summers: You have come to know the site very well and have watched it develop over the months. What was your main aim when thinking about the planting scheme?

David Richardson: Simplicity is the key to the planting layout and we have always given assurances to our neighbours in Fromelles that we will not plant a screen of trees. The trees will mature with the cemetery. The planting in the bastions around the Cross will be strong architectural forms to enhance the shape of the Cross terrace and to contrast with the creamy Massangies stone used for the paving and the Cross of Sacrifice. The site itself is slightly elevated looking towards V.C. Corner and the Cobbers Memorial. It is a wonderful location for a cemetery. It was clear from early discussions with the mayor and people of Fromelles that they

wanted a cemetery that was part of the village. The horticulture complements the design of the site. The form of the cemetery is strong and the colour contrasts between the red brick, the cream coloured stone and the turf will be very beautiful. In many ways the flowering plants in the borders will be a bonus in spring and summer.

Julie Summers: What are your thoughts about this project now that it has reached completion?

David Richardson: Well, our job will continue of course. That is the nature of the Commission's work. However, not only have we laid these men to rest with respect and dignity but we have created a whole new cemetery, which adds to the Commonwealth War Grave Commission's heritage. I count myself immensely lucky to have overseen the project from the very start.

The Funeral Ceremonies

Julie Summers

On a bitterly cold day in February 21 men were laid to rest in the new cemetery at Fromelles. These were individual ceremonies put on not for the benefit of visitors but in honour and remembrance of the men to be buried there that day. Julie Summers watched the funerals.

On this occasion the burial parties comprised soldiers from the Royal Regiment of Fusiliers and the Australian Army. Three each side of each coffin and a sergeant and padre, one party with Australian padre burying on the left hand side of the cemetery facing the cross, the other with the British padre, burying on the right hand side.

All beautifully ordered and organised. One burial at a time, each coffin treated with the same reverence, respect and honour.

"I'm convinced we're doing the right thing," Major Jason Kerr of the Australian Army said. "These men would have wanted to have been buried by their peers. And that is what we are doing for them now, albeit 93 years later. Time does not matter. Once you are a soldier you are part of that family and it never changes."

The Fusiliers agreed. Captain Matthew Clarke said, "It's an absolute privilege to be doing this work. We are honouring our brothers-in-arms. We feel so lucky to be able to take part in this important ceremony."

As the coffins were lowered into the ground and the padres intoned familiar and moving lines the spindrift whipped up in a fury around the walls of the cemetery. Two members of the Royal British Legion stood upon the terrace in front of the Cross of Sacrifice throughout each burial, raising and lowering their standard. Not a move was out of place. This was respect at its most precise. But it was deeply moving.

Nothing can take away from the fact that the men buried here have been missing since 1916 and their parents and families had no idea where they lay. Now they have been accorded the respect they deserve.

Australian Padre Catie Inches-Ogden said, "When the sergeant is about to call his coffin bearers to march I look down at each coffin I have committed and I think of the mothers and fathers who never knew where their sons were buried. I think the significance of what we are doing here in Fromelles will sink in with time but I feel privileged to be here."

British Padre Patrick Irwin felt equally fortunate. "The service we conduct is the service that would have been read over the coffins of those buried in the Great War. We're doing for these men now what they would have done for their mates 90 plus years ago."

At the end of the day the sun broke through the clouds and a small group of visitors gathered at the cemetery to witness the Close of Day. Twenty-one men had been laid to rest. The visitors left, as did the Royal Fusiliers, who were replaced by men of 4th Rifles, but the burial parties continued every other day for the following week until their work was completed, their work to honour their brothers-in-arms.

opposite below right
This bugle, used by the Australians to sound Last Post in the opening and closing ceremonies at Fromelles in 2010, was presented to the 31st Battalion AIF by Mr A. J. Cotton of Hidden Vale, Grandchester in August 1915

above A Firing Party
at the closing ceremony
on 10 February 2010

below Major Jason Kerr
signing off the burials
for that day

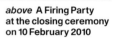

Who Were These Men?

Julie Summers

In order to give a flavour of the men behind the story, four family members talked to Julie Summers about their soldiers and explained what it means to be caught up in this story nearly a century after the Battle of Fromelles.

So far in this book we have explored the history and science behind the discovery of the bodies at Fromelles, and the architecture of remembrance constructed above their final resting place. But the question remains: who were these men? We know they came from Britain and Australia and we know that they had been in France only a matter of weeks. We also know they were aged from their teens to mid-forties. But whose sons, brothers, husbands or lovers were they? That is something that has to be fitted together carefully using all the various pieces of the puzzle that calls itself 'identification'; for each individual soldier this process also touches on a personal family history.

Bronwyn Owens from New South Wales knew nothing about her great-uncle, Douglas Caswell, until she began to research her family tree in early 2008. It was only then that she discovered that her maternal grandmother, Nellie McLennan, had had a brother who had been killed in the First World War.

"I guess my mother and her siblings all knew about their mother's brother dying in WWI, but they have all now died and the next generation, we kids, had no idea about any family connections."

Bronwyn Owens' interest in her family's history would soon take her and the rest of the family on a remarkable journey to help rediscover and honour one of the many men lost in the horror of Fromelles.

In May 2008, an article appeared in Bronwyn's local paper, the *Newcastle Morning Herald* in which her aunt, who had been married to her mother's brother, revealed that she was in possession of the identity tags of one Private Douglas Caswell (30th Battalion) AIF. The tags had been returned to his parents via the Red Cross in 1917. Bronwyn's aunt, Beth McLennan, had also been asked to help find a blood relative of Caswell to provide a DNA sample. Private Caswell was known from military records to have been killed in the Battle of Fromelles. The combination of his dog tags as proof that the Germans buried him and the contemporary evidence that placed him close to the front line in the battle, makes him a member of the so-called 191 group who might be among those found at Fromelles in 2009. This surprising piece of news came via email just a day or so after the article appeared in the newspaper so that

opposite Men of the 53rd Battalion waiting to attack at Fromelles. Only three of these men survived, all were wounded

below Private Caswell's disc was returned to his parents almost a year after he was killed at Fromelles

Bronwyn had hardly had time to digest one piece of information before the next followed.

Even the remote possibility that her great-uncle might be identified, catapulted Bronwyn and her family into a new and extraordinary scene being played out over half a world away. The setting shifted to Upton-upon-Severn in Worcestershire. Bronwyn discovered that her grandfather Edwin Caswell, a coal agent from Worcestershire, had emigrated to Australia with his son, Douglas, in 1912. Sophie Caswell and her daughter Nellie, Bronwyn's grandmother, arrived the following year. Bronwyn's cousin, Deborah Carrigan, made a trip to Worcester to see for herself where their family had come from. Not only had a local journalist, Richard Vernalls, made arrangements for a tour of the area but he had also organised for them to meet a family member who still lives in the village of Powick.

"It was a very moving visit," Deborah explained. "To have walked the lanes where my grandmother and Douglas may have played, to travel the same road and to explore the streets of Worcester was an experience that becomes more meaningful as time passes. Also, I am particularly interested that Sophie Caswell was of German descent, from Wiesbaden. I can only imagine the family discussions that must have gone on before he enlisted," she said.

Long before the story of Douglas Caswell came to light, Bronwyn had planned to be in France to celebrate her 60th birthday on 21 July 2010. "This will be my seventh trip to France. Subconsciously there must be a link to my being a Francophile. My daughter Brittany and her husband Grant and their two sons, Ethan and Joshua will be there with me at the unveiling ceremony. Third

and fourth generations. When I originally planned this holiday, I had no idea that I would (and I dearly hope this is the case) be celebrating the life and death of my great uncle at his grave. I sincerely pray that Douglas' remains are discovered and that finally he will be laid to rest, not as an unknown soldier but identified by a headstone and honoured by the fact that he gave his life so that his relations, present day and future ones, will know his story and be able to visit his grave. This whole adventure has made me recognise Douglas as a whole person who had his life cut short fighting for what he thought was the right thing to do."

Deborah concurs: "I feel that with my trip to Douglas' birthplace and Bronwyn's trip to France where Douglas's life ended so tragically, we are paying homage to his life, and giving him an enduring heritage and respect."

above **Caswell's identity disc is the only known object that belonged to him in the family's collection**

opposite **Private Alexander Stanley Clingan**

Margaret Wright knew more about her extended family than Bronwyn Owens but she too has been swept along by the events at Fromelles. Her distant cousin, Alexander Stanley Clingan, was killed on 19 July 1916 and, like Douglas Caswell, is also a member of the group of 191.

Margaret travelled a great deal during her twenties, hitch-hiking from London to Moscow via Marrakesh in the mid-1960s. "Through all these years, since childhood in fact, I maintained my interest in my family history, jotting down names, places and anecdotes. Clingan is rather an unusual name and wherever I am, I scan memorials for the name. We believe that all the Clingans in Australia are descended from the first arrivals in 1853."

The Clingan family history was not straightforward: "Because of a family schism in about 1920, I was unable to gain any oral history. Grandma was not talking. She even pasted the front pages of the family bible together so successfully that, try as we might, even today no conservator has been able successfully to unglue the pages for Clingan information."

The only details that Margaret could glean was that cousin Alex had died in Flanders on his 21st birthday in 1915. Then, just after the turn of this century Margaret was walking along the main street in Newtown, in Sydney when she saw an imposing war memorial outside an old school. There were 600 names. "As usual, I scanned them," she said. "And there, for the first time in a lifetime of scanning every memorial in every country and town I have ever been in, was A.S. Clingan! I remembered the name from my family chart. Alexander S."

Margaret discovered, via the CWGC, that his name was commemorated on the memorial at V.C. Corner. This made her wonder what had become of him. He had died on Wednesday 19 July 1916 aged 22. "So from this record," she explained, "I found that he was not killed on his 21st birthday, nor was he in Flanders, and nor did he die in 1915."

Next, she contacted the Australian Archives to obtain the dossier on Alexander Stanley Clingan. "Here was a wealth of information from his signing up until Missing in Action, then finally Killed in Action. Then followed letters from his mother wanting news of his fate, his medals, and finally a death certificate so she could receive his pension."

Alex had signed up at the Victoria Barracks, NSW on 8 August, 1915. At the time he left Sydney he was living with his widowed mother, Ruth in Newtown. Private Alexander Clingan sailed first to Egypt and then, a month later, having been transferred to the 53rd Battalion at Tel-el-Kebir, left Alexandria on 19 June 1916 and arrived at Marseilles nine days later.

On Sunday 2 July he wrote to his mother from Thiennes, some 50km west of Lille. He described his journey through France by train and his delight at the sights he saw including the wild flowers and poppies growing in the fields and on the railway embankments. He went on: 'We are billeted in barns and sheds in a large village within hearing of the heavy guns in the firing line. The barn holds about 30 of us and at the back is a fair sized paddock. Yesterday evening a football was brought up and it wasn't long before sides were picked and they were tearing into us for all they were worth. It gets dark here about 9:30-10 o'clock.

'After tea last night we saw plenty of aeroplanes going up having a look at the enemy lines with shells bursting behind, in front, under and over but a devil a one could they hit. About 8:30 in the night a heavy firing started and lasted well into the early hours of the morning. It reminded us that there was a war on and not very far away either.'

Ten days later he wrote a postcard to his mother. It was to be the last communication he ever sent her: 'Just a line to let you know that I am O.K. We have shifted again nearer the firing. We are in houses in a village which presents a very dilapidated appearance. Only a few have windows intact and many have holes in the roof, slates off etc. We moved into this place late at night with guns going off and flares lighting up the trenches in front. We arrived alright, no one being hurt . . . along the road we passed one of our big guns . . . You could [see] the flash and feel the concussion . . .'.

When Margaret transcribed these words she put herself into the shoes of Alexander's mother. She says: "I shuddered as I read his words about hearing the firing and seeing the big guns and the flares and being within a mile of the firing line. It's as if he were obsessed by the idea of the firing line, as indeed all the poor boys probably were. In a way perhaps he was preparing her for what might happen".

The next communication from France came at the beginning of September. An 'Urgent Telegram' dated 30 August 1916 stated: 'Regret to inform you that No.3168 Pte A.S. Clingan 53rd, Late 1st Batt is officially reported missing 19th July. Should particulars be received you will be informed immediately'.

For a lonely widow in Newtown no news could have been more devastating. It was not until the following year that she received any further official information about the fate of her youngest son. As the mother of a son, Margaret could almost feel Ruth's pain as she read the final telegram dated 2 April 1917 sent via a Reverend Dinning in Alice Street, Newtown: 'Officially reported that number 3168 Pte A S Clingan 53rd Battalion previously reported missing now reported killed in action 19th July.'

For the next several months Ruth Clingan wrote letters trying to get a death certificate, her son's pension, his medals and finally, his memorial death plaque, more commonly known to the troops as the Dead Man's Penny. This represented the sum total of what remained of all but the memory of Private Alexander Clingan. Until 2009 that is.

Margaret Wright is hopeful that his remains will be found among those from which DNA has been taken at Fromelles: "It will be wonderful if each of the soldiers has his own grave with a headstone, even if not identified. For some, simply 'Known unto God' will be all that can be hoped for. It is always very special to be able to place a poppy on the grave of a known person, and to give Alexander Stanley Clingan a named grave after 95 years, means a great deal. I shall bring my poppy from Australia and remember Alex and his mother, Ruth, who never knew where her boy rested."

On the other side of the world a family in Scotland is piecing together the story of their relative lost in France. Private Henry Turnbull, 297305, from Denny near Stirling, was a keen cyclist and the story goes that he signed up at the beginning of the war because he wanted a bicycle. His father told the army that his son was under age for front-line duty and he received assurances that Henry would be joining a cycle corps, the Highland Cyclist Battalion, and delivering messages, so he would be nowhere near the fighting. Sadly for the family Henry was all too close to the fighting. He was transferred to the 2nd/7th Battalion, Royal Warwickshire Regiment and he was killed on 19 July 1916 at the age of seventeen.

left Letter from the Red Cross to Ruth Clingan, which starts: 'It is with the greatest regret that we have to inform you that our Agents in London have written to us to say that the above soldier's name appears in the German Death List issued on 4th November 1916.' It goes on to explain that the Germans had buried the bodies after obtaining the identity discs, thus leaving little doubt but 'that the above soldier must have died and we would ask you to accept from all of us our sincerest sympathy in your great sorrow.' The letter is dated March 1917

above Private Henry Turnbull of the Highland Cyclist Battalion in 1914. He was later transferred to the 2nd/7th Battalion Royal Warwickshire Regiment

opposite left Private Henry Turnbull and his older brother, William

opposite right The last letter written by Henry Turnbull to his sister from France in 1916

Henry Turnbull was the youngest of eleven children, born in July 1898, 22 years after his oldest sister, Barbara. His great-great nephew, *Andrew MacDougall*, descended from Agnes, the third daughter of the Turnbull family, began doing research into the family history after his grandmother, Margaret Sutherland Jarvie, Agnes's daughter, died in 1997. He regretted not asking more questions and as he began to piece together his family tree, he found among other papers of interest, a letter from the trenches written by Henry Turnbull, a man he had never heard of before. The envelope that contained the letter also held a handful of photographs that helped Andrew to identify Henry's regiment and establish that he was commemorated on the Loos Memorial in France.

It was not until the spring of 2009 that the name Henry Turnbull cropped up again and this time it was in connection with the story of the Fromelles finds. One of Andrew's cousins, Bob Crilly, who had been researching Henry Turnbull's military record, contacted him to say that he had registered his details with the Australian group looking into the history of the battle at Fromelles. Andrew, as the only family member with direct information about Henry, in the form of the letter and photographs, became the hub of a large extended family, many of whom have provided information about the Turnbull siblings but little more about the young man himself.

The letter from Henry Turnbull was written from the trenches not long after he landed in France in June 1916. It was addressed to 'Dear Sister' and he writes about the horror of the shelling: 'I know what they are like [the heavy shells], when they are coming over it is like hell upon earth but they don't keep it up for long but is bad enough. [It] has been raining for a few days ... the trenches are up to the boots' heads in muck.' He ends by asking her to write soon and wishes her goodnight, signing the letter Harry SWAK (sealed with a kiss). He asks to be remembered to 'little Willie, also Barbara and Maggie', the latter being Andrew's grandmother. It is probably the last letter he ever wrote.

Andrew MacDougall added: "While it is sad to think that so very little is known about Uncle Henry, it is nevertheless comforting to know that he might be among those buried in the new cemetery at Fromelles. We are happy that Henry will finally be laid to rest with the dignity he deserves and that even though he was from a fairly poor working class background, he is now being given recognition and a respectful burial."

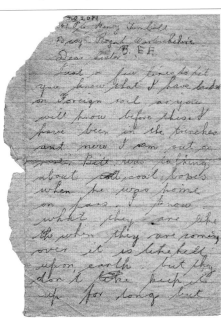
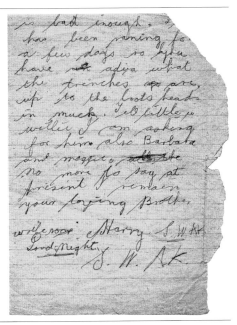

Unlike the three young men above, whose life stories have been rediscovered, Private Benjamin James or Uncle Benny was a very big presence in the life of *James Powell* when he was growing up in South Wales in the 1920s. Benny was one of five sons and seven daughters, the youngest of whom was James's mother. Eighteen months after James was born in 1925 his father died and he and his mother moved back to live with his maternal grandparents in their family home in Merthyr Tydfil and that is where he learned all about Uncle Benny, who had died in the Great War.

Born in October 1891, Benjamin James was 22 at the outbreak of the war. He signed up immediately, although he held a job – as an engine driver at a colliery – that might have excluded him from war service. By May 1916 he was in France with the Royal Warwickshires and just under two months later, at the age of 24, he was dead. At first his parents clung to the hope that he had been taken prisoner by the Germans. The notice Missing in Action was received in 1916 but it was not until 1921, when his medals were returned to them, that they gave up all hope that their son was still alive.

"It was very sad for my grandparents," James Powell says. "They died not knowing how their son had died nor where he was buried. They knew simply that he had been missing in 1916."

Benjamin James appears to have been something of a daredevil and a family legend. James remembered his grandfather telling him that Uncle Benny had been a fitness fanatic and a body builder. He kept the Indian clubs (popular for exercise in the late nineteenth- and early twentieth century) that Benny had used for his exercise as well as the books he had read on body building. James also remembers his grandfather talking

about seeing Benny diving off cliffs into the sea in Pembrokeshire on a family holiday before the war.

In 1956, James moved to Maidenhead in Berkshire, where he was appointed Borough Librarian until he retired. On one occasion he was invited to lunch at the Commonwealth War Graves Commission's headquarters on Marlow Road, opened there in 1972, and it was then that he discovered when his uncle died: 19 July 1916, and where he was commemorated, namely on the Loos Memorial. A quarter of a century later, in March 2009, he heard news about the discoveries at Fromelles and the date of the battle rang a bell. He immediately telephoned the CWGC to ask if there were any members of the Warwickshires amongst those believed to be found at Fromelles. To his surprise he learned that his uncle's name was on the list of those who might

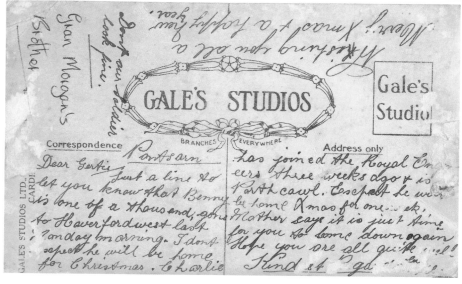

90

opposite Private
Benjamin James on
the front of a postcard,
on the verso of which
is a letter written by
one of his sisters to
another describing
him leaving for France.
'I don't expect he will be
home for Christmas',
she wrote

above Private Benjamin
James (centre, kneeling)
with unknown comrades,
probably in France

above right
A headstone to an
unknown soldier
buried at Fromelles
(Pheasant Wood)
Cemetery

possibly have been buried at Pheasant Wood.

"I went to France in November 2009 to see the place for myself," James said. "It was very wet and sticky underfoot and we got stuck in the mud. It really is as glutinous as they said it was in the books about the Great War."

He went on, "My grandparents spoke so much about their son, my uncle Benny. They would be so relieved if his remains were found and would be delighted if he could have a headstone. I have a grandson called Benjamin and if they identify Uncle Benny's body I should like to take him to the cemetery."

At the time of writing, none of the people interviewed for this essay knows whether or not their relative will be identified and named. Nevertheless the relief expressed by all of them that an individual grave, and perhaps one day a named headstone, reminds one of the great cost of war.

Andrew MacDougall sums up his own feelings, which seem to reflect the general mood amongst the relatives of those believed to be buried at Fromelles: "Personally, I am excited to have found in our family what I can only describe as a hero. A brave lad that stepped forward when he was only 15, although he absolutely didn't have to. Knowing that there is a chance that Henry may be found gives me a great deal of satisfaction. My grandmother and her mother would never have imagined what a fuss has been made of Henry now and how, through that, his memory has been perpetuated."

Postscript: In March 2010 Private Alexander Stanley Clingan was named as one of 75 soldiers positively identified. An inscribed headstone was erected above his grave to the delight and pride of his family in Australia.

Index

Acknowledgements

The Commonwealth War Graves Commission would like to extend warms thanks to individuals and organisations who have worked towards the successful realisation of one of the largest projects undertaken by the Commission in recent years and to all those who have helped bring this commemorative publication and accompanying exhibition together.

Photographic acknowledgements

Daniel Alexander p. 71; Australian War Memorial pp. 14 (E05590), 16 (detail of J03376, E03969), 17 (E04044), 18 (H16396, A01551), 19 (C01409, A01652), 20 (A01566), 23 (P06285), 84 (A03042), 87 (P05301.032);
Kate Brady pp. 34-55, 67
Caswell family pp. 85-6
Clingan family p. 88
Damon Cleary Imperial War Museum pp. 79 (IWM_LOC_2010_001_074), 80 top (IWM_LOC_2010_001_173), 80 middle (IWM_LOC_2010_001_208), 80 bottom left (IWM_LOC_2010_001_732), 80 bottom right (IWM_LOC_2010_001_861), 81 top right (top right, IWM_LOC_2010_001_793), 81 middle right (IWM_LOC_2010_001_794), 81 bottom right (IWM_LOC_2010_001_267); 82 top left (IWM_LOC_2010_001_883), 82 bottom left (IWM_LOC_2010_001_640), 82 bottom right (IWM_LOC_2010_001_973)
James family pp. 90-91
Ordnance Survey 1936 p. 15
Tim Loveless pp. 21 (top), 26, 27, 30-33, 56-59, 62, 66
Jean-Pierre Pepek, Balloide Photo pp. 28, 70
Tony Pollard pp. 24, 25
Julie Summers pp. 78, 80 (top right) 82 (top right)
Turnbull family pp. 88-89
Roland Wessling p. 29
Chloe Wootten pp. 81 (top left, bottom left), 82 (middle left), 83

All remaining historical images were supplied by the Commonwealth War Graves Commission. Recent images of Fromelles other than those listed above were taken by CWGC staff

Remembering Fromelles

First published in 2010 by CWGC Publishing

Commonwealth War Graves Commission
2 Marlow Road, Maidenhead, Berkshire SL6 7DX

Remembering Fromelles © 2010 CWGC Publishing
Texts © 2010 the authors

ISBN-13: 978-0956507402

Designed by Untitled
www.untitledstudio.com

Origination, printing and binding by
Manor Creative, Eastbourne
www.manorcreative.com

Printed using vegetable based inks on paper from well-managed forests

Mixed Sources
Product group from well-managed forests and other controlled sources
www.fsc.org Cert no. TT-COC-002794
© 1996 Forest Stewardship Council
FSC

front cover Detail of Cobbers by Peter Corlett. The statue was erected in 1998 in memory of those who fought and fell in the Battle of Fromelles and depicts Sergeant Simon Frasier of the 57th Battalion whose company brought in many wounded men from the battlefield. Photograph by Hans de Regt

back cover Fromelles (Pheasant Wood) Cemetery photograph David Richardson; Archaeology and Finds photographs Tim Loveless